ALSO BY JON WINOKUR

ZEN
TO GO

BITE-
SIZED
BITS
OF
WISDOM

Compiled & Edited by
JON WINOKUR
Author of **THE PORTABLE CURMUDGEON**

SASQUATCH BOOKS
SEATTLE

To the memory of Tobi Sanders

Printed in Canada
Published by Sasquatch Books
Distributed by Publishers Group West
13 12 11 10 09 08 07 06 05   6 5 4 3 2 1

Cover illustration: Greg Clarke
Book design: Kate Basart/Union Pageworks

Library of Congress Cataloging-in-Publication Data
Zen to go / compiled and edited by Jon Winokur
        p. cm.
        Includes bibliographical references and index.
        ISBN 1-57061-447-4
        1. Zen Buddhism—Quotations, maxims, etc.
        I. Winokur, Jon

BQ9267.Z475 2005
294.3'927—dc22   2005042562

Sasquatch Books | 119 South Main Street, Suite 400
Seattle, WA 98104 | 206/467-4300
www.sasquatchbooks.com | custserv@sasquatchbooks.com

CONTENTS

ACKNOWLEDGMENTS

From *Questions to a Zen Master* by Taisen Deshimaru, translated and edited by Nancy Amphoux. ©1961 by Zen ed. Retz, English translation ©1985 by E. P. Dutton, Inc. Reprinted by permission of the publisher, E. P. Dutton, a division of NAL Penguin, Inc.

From *The Ring of the Way: The Testament of a Zen Master* by Taisen Deshimaru. ©1983 by Editions Cesare Rancilio. English translation ©1987 by E. P. Dutton, Inc. Reprinted by permission of the publisher, E. P. Dutton, a division of NAL Penguin, Inc.

From *The Zen Way to the Martial Arts* by Taisen Deshimaru, translated by Nancy Amphoux. ©1983 by Taisen Deshimaru. Reprinted by permission of the publisher, E. P. Dutton, a division of NAL Penguin, Inc.

From *Zen and the Art of Motorcycle Maintenance* by Robert Pirsig, ©1974 by Robert Pirsig. Reprinted by permission of the publisher, William Morrow and Company, Inc.

INTRODUCTION

Six centuries before the birth of Christ, a young prince named Gautama Siddhartha lived in a palace on the slopes of the Himalayas in what is now Nepal. According to legend, he led an opulent, sheltered life until the day he left the palace for the first time. While traveling with a servant, he saw an old woman and discovered that people grow old and infirm; he saw a sick child and learned of the existence of disease; he encountered a funeral procession and for the first time confronted mortality. Finally he met a grinning, half-naked beggar. "How can this man smile in the face of such misery?" Gautama asked his servant. "He's smiling because he's a holy man. He's enlightened," the servant replied. His peace of mind shattered, with a yearning for liberation from worldly suffering and an unaccountable sense of destiny, Gautama renounced his patrimony and left the palace in search of enlightenment.

For seven years he wandered about India without success. Finally he sat down under a fig tree near Gaya and vowed to stay there until he had attained enlightenment. On the seventh day he opened his eyes, saw the morning star, and had a Great Awakening in which he grasped Ultimate

Reality. Liberated from all worldly pain and illusion, he had become the *Buddha*, the Enlightened One. For the next forty-nine years he traveled up and down India preaching the doctrine that is the foundation of Buddhism.

The Buddha taught that the ego, or "self," is the cause of all suffering. In its frantic pursuit of comfort and security, it imprisons us in a vicious cycle of joy and pain, because comfort and security are illusions. In an effort to promote its separate existence, the grasping self alienates us from our original condition of oneness with the Absolute and condemns us to a life of delusion.

We try to ease the pain of separation from our true nature by resorting to what the Buddha called the "five thieves": sex, gluttony, pursuit of status, greed, and insanity. We take refuge in ultimately meaningless activity. We deify the intellect and denigrate the mystical. We seek but we never find, because the intellect is useless for realizing Ultimate Truth. We're out of sync with the cosmos because we experience life through a veil of duality, wrongly discriminating between subject and object, mind and body, observer and observed. We're born free from such delusion, but as we're gradually "educated," the self grows, takes control, and isolates us from our true nature.

By means of *zazen*, a special form of sitting meditation, and *sanzen*, the interplay between master and student, Zen awakens us from our "cultural trance," silences the self, and returns us to our original state of grace.

The Buddha left no writings. After his death disciples passed down his teachings orally, but eventually scriptures were compiled, monks and nuns were ordained, and monasteries sprang up throughout India. Zen, a school of Buddhism strongly influenced by Taoism, developed in China in the sixth century AD and was eventually brought to Japan. (*Zen* is the Japanese word for "meditation.") By the beginning of this century, Zen had taken root in the West, where it has flourished since the end of World War II.

Zen is not a religion. It offers no heaven, no hell, no sin, no guilt, no miracles, no sacraments, no saints. Zen is not ritualistic, dogmatic, or sanctimonious. Zen is not a cult: It doesn't proselytize, preach, or moralize. It doesn't explain or promote itself. Although it has "masters" and "students," strictly speaking there is nothing to teach and nothing to learn. Zen defies analysis: The harder you try to understand it, the more elusive it becomes. As the maxim says, "When you seek it, you cannot find it."

Zen isn't a moral philosophy; it avoids metaphysical speculation and focuses on the concrete. Its goal is experience, not understanding. It deals not with constructs and symbols of life, but with life itself. Zen is eminently practical, giving its adherents a way of living their lives, a way of being in the world, a way of doing ordinary things (hence the many "Zen in the Art of . . ." books).

Because Zen involves a personal experience, an epiphany, many of the books about Zen published in English have addressed the problem of describing the ineffable. These books customarily have disclaimers to the effect that no amount of writing or talking *about* Zen can communicate its essence, because Ultimate Truth cannot be dragged down to the level of mere language. A book about Zen is thus a paradox, in the same way that "words can describe a glass of water, but they cannot quench your thirst" or "the finger pointing at the moon is not the moon itself."

It's true that language is inherently dualistic and categorical, and just as the finger is not the moon, this book is not Zen. It doesn't presume to explain Zen, but can only hint at the experience at Zen's heart and beckon the reader beyond the printed word toward that experience. Even though reading is the epitome of discursive thinking, it's a first step: I first learned of Zen in the writings of D. T. Suzuki, R. H. Blyth, Eugen Herrigel, Taisen Deshimaru, Shunryu Suzuki, Alan Watts, Thomas Merton, and Peter Matthiessen.

Many books about Zen also contend that Zen is better suited to the Eastern mind because the traditional Western world view reduces nature to fundamental units and divides spirit from matter, while in the East nature is seen as one unified, harmonious whole. Western rationalism is thus set against Eastern mysticism: an ordered, mechanistic universe versus a nonrational, mystical one.

The idea that the spirit of Zen resides exclusively in the East is un-Zen-like and is precisely the kind of dualistic thinking that Zen rejects. In reality, the wisdom of Zen resonates with countless expressions of Western culture, with its theology and philosophy, even with the "New Physics"— *especially* with the New Physics, which has replaced the classical view of a clockwork cosmos with the conception of an indivisible whole in which no part is more important than another.

If Zen teaches anything, it's that Zen is not confined to the East or to Japan. It isn't confined to Buddhism. It lives in the arts, in sports, in the most routine aspects of daily life. Zen is everywhere.

Here are expressions of the spirit of Zen in the words not only of Zen masters, but also of Western philosophers, theologians, mystics, artists, scientists, businessmen, and athletes. Such diverse sages as Meister Eckhart, Jung, Wittgenstein, Bertrand Russell, Aldous Huxley, John Cage, Ray Kroc, even Yogi Berra—*especially* Yogi Berra—have all eloquently demonstrated their Zen.

Zen is simple and unpretentious. It's friendly. It doesn't take itself too seriously. It doesn't sit on its behind in some shrine, it gets out and mingles. It's flexible and portable, but it isn't junk food for the soul, it's hearty spiritual nourishment. It has dignity, a sense of humor, and a gritty, iconoclastic spirit. This book is meant to convey that spirit.

—J. W.

Pacific Palisades, California

ZEN ABUSE

Garage sale day.

It was a real "Zen-o-thon"—we decided the time had arrived to shake ourselves of all our worldly crap and become minimalists—or at least try starting from scratch again—more psychic pioneering.

"This is so 'Zenny,'" Bug said happily, as some poor cretin purchased his used electric razor (ugh!) as well as his collection of Elle MacPherson merchandise.

Douglas Coupland, *Microserfs*

There's been a disturbing trend of late: the trivialization of Zen, either to claim enlightenment, or to lend cachet to a commercial product. This cavalier use of Zen, now epidemic, was identified and dubbed "Zen abuse" by Peter Bell in a 1998 *Icon Magazine* article:

> Enlightenment is figured as a free high, a doorway to a higher state of consciousness, like a psychedelic, and just as drugs are abused, Zen is abused. With glazed eyes and a strand of spittle hanging down his chin, the meditating Hollywood agent, personal Zen master at his side, sits in ecstatic union with the universe. But real Zen is eminently worldly. Enlightenment and its supposed ethereal

splendor is not the end of Zen but the beginning. The Zen master gets off his holy ass, leaves the monastery, and hobbles into town like a vagabond with all his worldly possessions on a stick, ready to alleviate the plight of the downtrodden. The Buddha set out to end suffering, not to bring focus to his tennis game. The Zen master doesn't sit on his $40 million compound forgetting the worries of Silicon Valley. The detached, meditating monk aims to become a Bodhisattva, a humble do-gooder. How many rock stars, basketball coaches, and captains of industry study Zen in the hopes that they will ditch their earthly possessions to aid street urchins? Probably as many as who convert to Judaism for the circumcision.

Zen is indeed Big in Hollywood, where it is lumped with, and contaminated by, such New Agery as trance channeling, healing crystals, aromatherapy, and the well-publicized dabbling in the Kabbalah by Gentile divas and divettes, one of whom also reportedly consults a pet psychic to learn whether her deceased dog has been reincarnated; where Barbra Streisand anoints tennis star André Agassi a "Zen master"; where k.d. lang conflates Zen with channeling ("Performing is like being possessed sometimes, because when I sing and it's really on and it's Zen, I have nothing to do with what's coming out. Honestly, I don't. All I do is provide the channel."); where Carrie Fisher pronounces Woody Allen a "Zen director"; and where the producer of *Terminator 2* reveals to the *Los Angeles Times* how he harnesses Zen as a productivity tool:

> The whole miracle of this stuff is that you can be more relaxed, calmer and yet get more done and have more energy. I'm less frantic. I don't scream as much as I used to. It's not how you take this stuff and retreat from the world; it's how you incorporate it into your daily life.

Zen abuse takes various linguistic forms, including the use of "Zen" as a modifier in the attempt to elevate ordinary activities. Thus: Zen golf, Zen tennis, Zen baseball, Zen poker, Zen driving, Zen screenwriting, Zen dating, Zen landscaping, Zen management, Zen cross-examination, Zen . . . farting (sic). The pairing of "Zen" with "the art of" also proceeds apace, going beyond Eugen Herrigel's *Zen in the Art of Archery* and Robert Pirsig's *Zen and the Art of Motorcycle Maintenance*, both of which showed that Zen can be properly and even poetically joined with other pursuits. The connections are increasingly tortured and artless, however, going beyond cooking, gardening, and mountain climbing to psychoanalysis, proposal writing, public relations, stand-up comedy, intravenous line placement, Hasidism, and, inevitably, the Internet (where, as might be expected, Zen abuse is rampant). It's one thing to write a book about Zen in the fiction of J. D. Salinger, another for the novelist Thomas Pynchon to equate Zen with channel surfing (both involve "nonlinear awareness," Pynchon says). Zen has even been likened to a horrible disease:

> Now I know this sounds way out there, but look at it this way: Alzheimer's is a detaching disease. It detaches people from their memories, their selves. We can look at that as tragic and awful, or we can change the frame. Consider Zen Buddhism, which is all about clearing your mind, detaching from your thoughts, grounding yourself in the moment. Well, that's Alzheimer's. (Kenneth Brummel-Smith, Department of Geriatrics, Florida State University College of Medicine)

Most egregious is the use of Zen to sell things. Marketeers may not be able to define Zen, but they think it sells. Hence the unholy alliance of Zen with innumerable products and services:

Zen Touch 20 Gigabyte MP3 Player

Zen Baby DVD for infants and toddlers [designed to] help create peace and well-being in the home and help young children unwind at the end of the day.

Lancome Hydra Zen Eye Skin De-Stressing Anti-Puffiness Eye Treatment (0.5 fl oz. for $39.50).

Zen Body Detergent: Be one with the bubbles . . . Suds away selfhood and excess ego with our scented body detergent. Let Zen free you from attachment and wordly desires (for stuff like fast cars and hotties and doughnuts and-oh, never mind) while scrubbing knees and elbows sparkling clean. Shower your way to Nirvana, and remember, just say "om" to dirt.

Trader Zen Home E-Zen-tials no-streak, multipur-pose cleaner with essential oils of cedarwood and sage in a 34-oz. squirt bottle.

Zen Garden Desktop Beach Set: Create your own desktop private beach retreat . . . brings the ocean surf to any room in your home or office. Incorpo-rates the ancient philosophy of relaxation & medi-tation with that great American pastime. Includes wood tray, lounge chair, beach umbrella with stand, beach ball, sandals and coolers.

Playtex Body Zen Soft Cup Bra

Commercial spaces are characterized as "Zen-like," which is how *Kitchen and Bath Design News* described a Manhattan appliance showroom, and how *Business Week* characterized Apple stores ("sleek, spacious, and staffed with highly trained sales associates. Interactions are meant to be soft-sell, and customers are encouraged to lounge on couches, take classes for non-geeks, or simply surf the Web"). The cable show *Divine Design* used the term to describe a bathroom:

> Jayne, Phil and their four children have lived in their 1920s home for over eight years. They have done lots of work to their house, but have left the master bedroom and bathroom in the same state as when they purchased the house. Their bathroom has been a communal one for the entire family, but Jayne and Phil have had enough and want it back. Host Candice Olson transforms the out-of-date bathroom into a Zen-like oasis that will be strictly off limits to the kids.

The loathsome "Zen vibe" has been used to describe everything from a driving range to bikini bottoms:

> Pebble [Beach] has a decent driving range a quick shuttle ride from the first tee, but one of the planet's most pleasant practice areas is just a mile down the road at Spyglass Hill. Warm up there and enjoy the Zen vibe of a range nestled among towering pines and grazing deer. (Alan Shipnuck, *Golf Magazine*, September 2004)

> Raisins Zen Vibe Low-Rise Bottoms: Big rectangular rings add earthy element to these hot bikini bottoms. (Internet ad)

In short, Zen has been tainted by countless glib associations. According to Peter Bell:

> "Zen" and "Zen-like" have come to mean everything from paradoxical, succinct, fleeting, and mysterious to serene, sage, and witty. For some reason, writers describe Zen-like cell phones and Zen surfing experiences, but never "Quaker-esque" or "Shinto-like" anything. . . . But even though people mean well when they use Zen as a metaphor, most often it is just a convenient hiding place for what may once have been called, say, irrational or flaky.

So beware. Though Zen is friendly and versatile and has a sense of humor, it isn't *flaky*. Though self-proclaimed Zen teachers abound like so many personal trainers of the spirit, Zen mastery is achieved only after rigorous, often lifelong practice. Though Zen is ordinary and practical and lives in virtually every facet of life, it is rarely found in advertising copy, because Zen doesn't *endorse*. And the only Zen you'll find in the new Calvin Klein flagship store is the Zen you bring with you.

A special transmission outside the Scriptures;
No dependence upon words and letters;
Direct pointing to reality;
Seeing into one's own nature and realizing
Buddhahood.

BODHIDHARMA

There ain't no answer.
There ain't going to be any answer.
There never has been an answer.
That's the answer.

GERTRUDE STEIN

ZEN

ZEN

Before you study Zen, a bowl is a bowl
and tea is tea. While you are studying
Zen, a bowl is no longer a bowl and tea is
no longer tea. After you've studied Zen,
a bowl is again a bowl and tea is tea.

ZEN MAXIM

Too much study makes Zen too thin; too
much practice makes it too thick.

MASAO ABE

The only Zen you find on the tops of
mountains is the Zen you bring up there.

ROBERT PIRSIG

Zen *is a Japanese translation of a Chinese translation* (ch'an) *of the Sanskrit word* (dhyana) *for "meditation."*

The aim of Zen is enlightenment: the immediate, unreflected grasp of reality, without affective contamination and intellectualization, the realization of the relation of myself to the universe.

ERICH FROMM

Among the most remarkable features characterizing Zen are these: spirituality, directness of expression, disregard of form or conventionalism, and frequently an almost wanton delight in going astray from respectability.

D. T. SUZUKI

The term "Zen Buddhism" is generally used to mean a school of Buddhism based on Zen and teaching Zen, an established religion treated as a social organization comparable to other religious sects and schools. "Zen," however, is one of the basic components characterizing oriental thought, and as such has great influence not only in religion, but in various phases of culture. It develops our ideas, and builds our characters. It is wisdom based on religious experience directly connected with the very source of our existence.

ZENKEI SHIBAYAMA

Zen is consciousness unstructured by particular form or particular system, a trans-cultural, trans-religious, transformed consciousness.

THOMAS MERTON

Zen is a way of liberation, concerned not with discovering what is good or bad or advantageous, but what is.

ALAN WATTS

Zen teaches nothing; it merely enables us to wake up and become aware. It does not teach, it points.

D. T. SUZUKI

Zen Buddhism does not preach. Sermons remain words. It waits until people feel stifled and insecure, driven by secret longing.

EUGEN HERRIGEL

Zen holds that there is no god outside the universe who has created it and has created man. God—if I may borrow that word for a moment—the universe, and man are one indissoluble existence, one total whole. Only THIS—capital THIS—is.

NANCY WILSON ROSS

Zen is simply a voice crying, "Wake up! Wake up!"

MAHA STHAVIRA SANGHARAKSHITA

Studying about Zen should never be confused with practicing Zen, just as studying aesthetics should not be confused with being an artist.

T. P. SAKULIS

Zen insists on personal experience and insight. Being aware of the glibness of words, it stresses the showing of insight-understanding, the clear seeing and actual understanding of it.

IRMGARD SCHLOEGL

Zen is not interested in high-flown statements; it wants its pupil to bite his apple and not discuss it.

ANNE BANCROFT

The Diamond Sutra is a basic Buddhist text written in Sanskrit that prescribes practices for the attainment of Ultimate Wisdom. So called because it is deemed "indestructible."

There are three kinds of disciples: those who impart Zen to others, those who maintain the temples and shrines, and then there are the rice bags and the clothes hangers.

NYOGEN SENZAKI

Zen teaches us to discover the transcendental core of our own selves in an immediate and practical sense, to "taste" divine Being in the here-and-now.

KARLFRIED GRAF DÜRCKHEIM

Zen is like looking for the spectacles that are sitting on your nose.

ZEN MAXIM

Zen is . . . joyous iconoclasm which respects nothing and no one, particularly itself.

DAVID BRANDON

Zen is the way of complete self-realization; a living human being who follows the way of Zen can attain satori and then live a new life as Buddha.

ZENKEI SHIBAYAMA

Tokusan Sengan (782–865) lived in northern China, where he studied the sutras and became a respected Buddhist scholar. When he heard that a sect in southern China advocated a "transmission outside the scriptures," he got angry and vowed to "exterminate the Zen devils." He set out for the south with a copy of the Diamond Sutra in a large box. On his way

*he stopped at a tea house and ordered a snack
from the old woman there. Now, "snack" in
Chinese literally means "to light up the mind."
The old woman asked Tokusan what he had in
the box, and he told her it was the Diamond
Sutra. "Is that so?" said the woman. "Then
answer this question: If you want a snack to
light up your mind, which mind are you going
to light up?" The Diamond Sutra contains
a famous passage that says, "Past mind is
unattainable, present mind is unattainable,
future mind is unattainable." Tokusan knew
the passage well and could discourse about
it with great erudition, but when the old
woman challenged him to apply its wisdom
to a practical matter, he was at a loss. Thus
realizing the limits of scholarship, Tokusan
decided to embrace Zen instead of trying to
destroy it.*

The study of Zen is like drilling wood to make fire: the wisest course is to forge ahead without stopping.

HAKUIN

Zen aims at freedom but its practice is disciplined.

GARY SNYDER

Zen training is designed to break through to non-duality. This is the sole and only purpose of all Zen effort, and the effort must come from within. Fellow seekers and—with far greater skill—Zen masters will help to point the seeker in the right direction, but when all this help is given, the road of Zen is a road of "Do it yourself"—teach *yourself* Zen.

CHRISTMAS HUMPHRIES

Zen has no business with ideas.

D. T. Suzuki

In life as well as in art Zen never wastes energy in stopping to explain; it only indicates.

Alan Watts

If you wish to obtain an orthodox understanding of Zen, do not be deceived by others. Inwardly or outwardly, if you encounter any obstacles kill them right away. If you encounter the Buddha, kill him.

Rinzai

Zen has no secrets other than seriously thinking about birth-and-death.

Takeda Shingen

Zen is to have the heart and soul of a little child.

TAKUAN

To be a good Zen Buddhist it is not enough to follow the teaching of its founder; we have to experience the Buddha's experience.

D. T. SUZUKI

Sanzen *is the personal interaction between Zen master and student designed to allow the student to demonstrate his Zen—or lack of it—to the master. The face-to-face confrontation can involve verbal sparring, harsh reprimands, even corporal punishment.*

Zen functions in non-duality. The process of thought, of reasoning, takes place in the field of duality. It follows that no thinking will achieve Zen.

CHRISTMAS HUMPHRIES

Zen is practice, experience, life—not explaining, interpreting, investigating, quibbling. All talk, as the Chinese masters of old say, is at best a finger pointing at the moon. The finger is not the moon and cannot pull the moon down.

HEINRICH DUMOULIN

To have Zen is to be in a state of pure sensation. It is to be freed from the grip of concepts, to see through them. This is *not* the same as rejecting conceptual thinking. Thoughts and words are in the

world and are as natural as flowers. It is
a mistake therefore to think that Zen is
anti-intellectual.

ALAN KEIGHTLEY

In Zen the ego enters into God.
God enters into the ego. Both.

TAISEN DESHIMARU

Delusions and attachments consisting of
self-centered and conceptual thinking
obscure the living fact. The Zen path
is devoted to clearing away these
obstructions and seeing into true nature.

ROBERT AITKEN

The practice of Zen is forgetting the self in the act of uniting with something.

KOUN YAMADA

Zen is not some kind of excitement, but concentration on our usual everyday routine.

SHUNRYU SUZUKI

Zen enriches no one. There is no body to be found. The birds may come and circle for a while in the place where it is thought to be. But they soon go elsewhere. When they are gone, the "nothing," the "no-body" that was there, suddenly appears. That is Zen. It was there all the time, but the scavengers missed it, because it was not their kind of prey.

THOMAS MERTON

Koan *are spiritually instructive conundrums designed to force the student beyond logic to sudden illumination. There are some 1,700 koan, many of which are compiled in the* Hekiganroku *and the* Mumonkan.

Zen cannot be defined. It is not a "thing" to be surrounded or reflected by words. When the last word is trowelled into the prison it escapes and laughs away on the horizon.

DAVID BRANDON

ACTION

We are so anxious to achieve some particular end that we never pay attention to the psycho-physical means whereby that end is to be gained. So

far as we are concerned, any old means
is good enough. But the nature of the
universe is such that ends can never
justify the means. On the contrary, the
means always determine the end.

ALDOUS HUXLEY

The Way of the sage is to act but not to
compete.

LAO TZU

The great end of life is not knowledge
but action.

THOMAS HENRY HUXLEY

Action should culminate in wisdom.

BHAGAVAD GITA

Action is the only reality; not only reality but morality as well.

ABBIE HOFFMAN

Inaction may be the highest form of action.

JERRY BROWN

Work is prayer. Work is also stink. Therefore stink is prayer.

ALDOUS HUXLEY

Doing work which has to be done over and over again helps us recognize the natural cycles of growth and decay, of birth and death, and thus become aware of the dynamic order of the universe. "Ordinary" work, as the root meaning of the term indicates, is work that is in harmony with the order we perceive in the natural environment.

Fritjof Capra

Monotony is the law of nature. Look at the monotonous manner in which the sun rises. The monotony of necessary occupations is exhilarating and life-giving.

Gandhi

If something is boring after two minutes, try it for four. If still boring, try it for eight, sixteen, thirty-two, and so on. Eventually, one discovers that it is not boring but very interesting.

Zen maxim

The best part of one's life is the working part, the creative part. Believe me, I love to succeed. . . . However, the real spiritual and emotional excitement is in the doing.

GARSON KANIN

Enjoyment is not a goal, it is a feeling that accompanies important ongoing activity.

PAUL GOODMAN

People love chopping wood. In this activity one immediately sees results.

ALBERT EINSTEIN

I dread success. To have succeeded is to have finished one's business on earth, like the male spider who is killed by the female the moment he has succeeded in his courtship. I like a state of continual becoming, with a goal in front and not behind.

GEORGE BERNARD SHAW

A priest from a rival Buddhist sect attended one of Master Bankei's (1622–1693) lectures. When the large audience welcomed Bankei with enthusiastic applause, the priest could not contain his jealousy: "You are a fraud," he cried out. "You may be able to fool these peasants and make them do whatever you say, but I have no respect for you. Can you make me do what you say?"

"Come here and I will show you," Bankei replied. As the priest approached the lectern Bankei said, "Come over to the left." The priest went to the left. "On second thought, come to the right." The priest went to the right. "Good," said Bankei, "you have obeyed me well. Now sit down and shut up."

Do you know that disease and death must needs overtake us, no matter what we are doing? . . . What do you wish to be doing when it overtakes you? If you have anything better to be doing when you are so overtaken, get to work on that.

EPICTETUS

Our deeds determine us, as much as we determine our deeds.

GEORGE ELIOT

You cannot think your way to right action, you have to act your way to right thinking.

DAVID MILCH

Blessed is he who has found his work.
Let him ask no other blessedness.

THOMAS CARLYLE

Originality and the feeling of one's own
dignity are achieved only through work
and struggle.

FYODOR DOSTOEVSKY

If the building of a bridge does not
enrich the awareness of those who work
on it, then that bridge ought not to be
built.

FRANTZ FANON

Put your heart, mind, intellect and soul even to your smallest acts. This is the secret of success.

SWAMI SIVANANDA

Whatsoever thy hand findeth to do, do it with thy might; for there is no work, nor device, nor knowledge, nor wisdom, in the grave, wither thou goest.

ECCLESIASTES 9:10

When you do something, you should burn yourself completely, like a good bonfire, leaving no trace of yourself.

SHUNRYU SUZUKI

Behavior influences consciousness. Right behavior means right consciousness. Our attitude here and now influences the entire environment: our words, actions, ways of holding and moving ourselves, they all influence what happens around us and inside us. The actions of every instant, every day, must be right. . . . Every gesture is important. How we eat, how we put on our clothes, how we wash ourselves, how we go to the toilet, how we put our things away, how we act with other people, family, wife, work—how we are: totally, in every single gesture.

TAISEN DESHIMARU

Do every act of your life as if it were your last.

MARCUS AURELIUS

Flow with whatever may happen and let your mind be free: Stay centered by accepting whatever you are doing. This is the ultimate.

CHUANG TZU

The less effort, the faster and more powerful you will be.

BRUCE LEE

Slow is smooth and smooth is fast.

ANONYMOUS

To know and to act are one and the same.

SAMURAI MAXIM

Try not to localize the mind anywhere, but let it fill up the whole body, let it flow throughout the totality of your being. When this happens you use the hands where they are needed, you use the legs and eyes where they are needed, and no time or energy will go to waste.

TAKUAN

(ADVICE TO A SAMURAI WARRIOR)

Think with the whole body.

TAISEN DESHIMARU

Softness triumphs over hardness, feebleness over strength. What is more malleable is always superior over that which is immovable. This is the principle of controlling things by going along with them, of mastery through adaptation.

LAO TZU

He who has gained the secret of Aikido
has the universe in himself and can say,
"I am the universe." When an enemy tries
to fight with him, the universe itself, he
has to break the harmony of the universe.
Hence at the moment he has the mind to
fight with me, he is already defeated.

MOREHEI UYESHIBA

You can learn from an ordinary bamboo
leaf what ought to happen. It bends lower
and lower under the weight of snow.
Suddenly the snow slips to the ground
without the leaf having stirred. Stay like
that at the point of highest tension until
the shot falls from you. So, indeed, it
is: when the tension is fulfilled, the shot
must fall, it must fall from the archer like
snow from a bamboo leaf, before he even
thinks it.

EUGEN HERRIGEL

Mushin: *The total absence of discursive thought; a state in which the ego is forgotten and the individual is free to perform without concern for dualistic notions of good or bad, success or failure.* Mushin *is the essence of Zen martial arts.*

When archery is performed in a state of "no-thought" (*mushin*), which means the absence of *all* ego consciousness, the archer is free from inhibitions as he puts an arrow into his bow, stretches the string, lets his eye rest on the target and, when adjustment is correct, lets the arrow go. There is no feeling of good or bad, accomplishment or failure. This is the "everyday mind" arising from "no-mind," and it is the essence of all the Zen martial arts to remain in this state, with no thought of life or death.

ANNE BANCROFT

It goes without saying that as soon as one cherishes the thought of winning the contest or displaying one's skill in technique, swordsmanship is doomed.

TAKANO SHIGEYOSHI

Sometimes you reach a point of being so coordinated, so completely balanced, that you feel that you can do anything— anything at all. At times like this I find I can run up to the front of the board and stand on the nose when pushing out through a broken wave; I can goof around, put myself in an impossible position and then pull out of it, simply because I feel happy. An extra bit of confidence like that can carry you through, and you can do things that are just about impossible.

MIDGET FARRELLY

Angels can fly because they take themselves lightly.

G. K. CHESTERTON

I never blame myself when I'm not hitting. I just blame the bat and if it keeps up I change bats. . . . After all, if I know it isn't my fault when I'm not hitting, how can I get mad at myself?

YOGI BERRA

There is a common experience in Tai Chi of seemingly falling through a hole in time. Awareness of the passage of time completely stops, and only when you catch yourself, after five or ten minutes, or five or ten seconds, is there the realization that for that period of time the world *stopped*.

TOM HORWITZ AND SUSAN KIMMELMAN

It's Zen-like when you're going good.
You are the ball and the ball is you. It
can do you no harm. A common bond
forms between you and this white sphere,
a bond based on mutual trust. The ball
promises not to fly over too many walls
after you have politely served it up to
enemy hitters, and you assure it that you
will not allow those same batters to treat
the ball in a harsh or violent manner.
Out of this trust comes a power that
allows the pitcher to take control of what
otherwise might be an uncontrollable
situation.

BILL LEE

Concentration is not staring hard at
something. It is not *trying* to concentrate.

W. TIMOTHY GALLWEY

A player's effectiveness is directly related to his ability to be right there, doing that thing, in the moment. All the preparation he may have put into the game—all the game plans, analysis of movies, etc.—is no good if he can't put it into action when the time comes. He can't be worrying about the past or the future or the crowd or some other extraneous event. He must be able to respond in the here and now.

JOHN BRODIE

Mountains should be climbed with as little effort as possible and without desire. The reality of your own nature should determine the speed. If you become restless, speed up. If you become winded, slow down. You climb the mountain in an equilibrium between restlessness and exhaustion. Then, when you're no longer thinking ahead, each footstep isn't just a means to an end but a unique event in itself.

ROBERT PIRSIG

You completely ignore everything and just concentrate. You forget about the whole world and just . . . are part of the car and track. . . . It's a very special feeling. You're completely out of this world. There is nothing like it.

JOCHEN RINDT

You're involved in the action and vaguely aware of it, but your focus is not on the commotion but on the opportunity ahead. I'd liken it to a sense of reverie— not a dreamlike state but the somehow insulated state that a great musician achieves in a great performance. He's aware of where he is and what he's doing, but his mind is on the playing of his instrument with an internal sense of *rightness*—it is not merely mechanical, it is not only spiritual; it is something of both, on a different plane and a more remote one.

ARNOLD PALMER

When I play my best golf, I feel as if I'm in a fog . . . standing back watching the earth in orbit with a golf club in your hands.

MICKEY WRIGHT

Without my telling it to, the right [-hand punch] goes, and when it hits, there is this good feeling. . . . Something just right has been done.

INGMAR JOHANSSON

I wasn't worried about a perfect game going into the ninth. It was like a dream. I was going on like I was in a daze. I never thought about it the whole time. If I'd thought about it I wouldn't have thrown a perfect game—I know I wouldn't.

CATFISH HUNTER

When the identity is realized, I as swordsman see no opponent confronting me and threatening to strike me. I seem to transform myself into the opponent, and every movement he makes as well as every thought he conceives are felt as if they were my own and I intuitively . . . know when and how to strike him.

D. T. SUZUKI

The body moves naturally, automatically, unconsciously, without any personal intervention or awareness. But if we begin to use our faculty of reasoning, our actions become slow and hesitant. Questions arise, the mind tires, and the consciousness flickers and wavers like a candle flame in a breeze.

TAISEN DESHIMARU

In Judo, he who thinks is immediately thrown. Victory is assured to the combatant who is both physically and mentally nonresistant.

ROBERT LINSSEN

Thinking . . . is what gets you caught from behind.

O. J. SIMPSON

How can you think and hit at the same time?

YOGI BERRA

ART

Correct handling of flowers refines the personality.

BOKUYO TAKEDA

If one really wishes to be master of an art, technical knowledge is not enough. One has to transcend technique so that the art becomes an "artless art" growing out of the Unconscious.

D. T. SUZUKI

The Zen ways and arts draw a bridge from real artistic creation (in painting, architecture, poetry) to artistic skills like flower arrangement and gardening, and ultimately to all of everyday life. The religious is found in the everyday, the sacred in the profane; indeed, the everyday is religious, the profane is sacred.

HEINRICH DUMOULIN

Archery, fencing, spear fighting, all the martial arts, tea ceremony, flower arranging . . . in all of these, correct breathing, correct balance, and correct stillness help to remake the individual. The basic aim is always the same: by tirelessly practicing a given skill, the student finally sheds the ego with its fears, worldly ambitions, and reliance on subjective scrutiny—sheds it so completely that he becomes the instrument of a deeper power, from which mastery falls instinctively, without further effort on his part, like a ripe fruit.

Wabi *means spare, impoverished; simple and functional. It connotes a transcendence of fad and fashion. The spirit of* wabi *imbues all the Zen arts, from calligraphy to karate, from the tea ceremony to Zen archery.*

The Zen way of calligraphy is to write in the most straightforward, simple way as if you were a beginner, not trying to make something skillful or beautiful, but simply writing with full attention as if you were discovering what you were writing for the first time; then your full nature will be in your writing.

SHUNRYU SUZUKI

Haiku is a particularly Zen form of poetry; for Zen detests egoism in the form of calculated effects or self-glorification of any sort. The author of haiku should be absent, and only the haiku present.

ANNE BANCROFT

A haiku is the expression of a temporary enlightenment in which we see into the life of things.

R. H. BLYTH

The Way of Tea lies in studying the ceremony, in understanding the principles, and in grasping the reality of things. These are its three rules.

Hosokawa Tadaoki

The art of the tea Way consists simply of boiling water, preparing tea and drinking it.

Rikyu

The essential art of Zen is *Sumi.*
Brush painting with ink on rice paper. It is wonderfully flexible, capable of both the most robust and delicate of forms. But what makes it most truly *Zen* is the clarity with which it conveys the mind of the painter. The first stroke is the final stroke; there are no touch-ups.

The Zen painter approaches his art as a part of his practice, as contemplation: Canvas blank, mind empty.

This art conveys the unity of Being and Action that leads to enlightenment. To freedom.

MICHAEL GREEN

Everything ultimately depends on what is outside and beyond the opposites, on the spirit, and on man's capacity not only to dissolve himself in it through passionate self-immersion, but also to live out of it with equal composure.

GUSTIE L. HERRIGEL

There is a certain point of unity within
the self, and between the self and its
world, a certain complicity and magnetic
mating, a certain harmony, that
conscious mind and will cannot direct.
Perhaps analysis and the separate mastery
of each element are required before the
instincts are ready to assume command,
but only at first. Command by instinct
is swifter, subtler, deeper, more
accurate, more in touch with reality
than command by conscious mind. The
discovery takes one's breath away.

MICHAEL NOVAK

If one is master of one thing and
understands one thing well, one has
at the same time, insight into and
understanding of many things.

VINCENT VAN GOGH

There is
one art,
no more,
no less;
to do
all things
with art-
lessness.

PIET HEIN

ILLUSION

ILLUSION

The foolish reject what they see, not what they think; the wise reject what they think, not what they see.

Huang Po

Five senses; an incurably abstract intellect; a haphazardly selective memory; a set of preconceptions and assumptions so numerous that I can never examine more than a minority of them—never become even conscious of them all. How much of total reality can such an apparatus let through?

C. S. Lewis

As in Rome there is, apart from the Romans, a population of statues, so apart from this real world there is a world of illusion, almost more potent, in which most men live.

JOHANN WOLFGANG VON GOETHE

What one believes to be true either is true or becomes true within limits to be found experientially and experimentally. These limits are beliefs to be transcended.

JOHN LILLY

I hate to be near the sea, and to hear it raging and roaring like a wild beast in its den. It puts me in mind of the everlasting efforts of the human mind, struggling to be free and ending just where it began.

WILLIAM HAZLITT

A great deal of intelligence can be
invested in ignorance when the need for
illusion is deep.

SAUL BELLOW

I think I think; therefore, I think I am.

AMBROSE BIERCE

Descartes said, "I think, therefore I am."
I say, "I do not think, that is why I exist."

TAISEN DESHIMARU

When one sees that everything exists
as an illusion, one can live in a higher
sphere than ordinary man.

THE BUDDHA

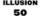

One may explain water, but the mouth
will not become wet. One may expound
fully on the nature of fire, but the mouth
will not become hot.

TAKUAN

This one life has no form and is empty
by nature. If you become attached by
any form, you should reject it. If you see
an ego, a soul, a birth, or a death, reject
them all.

BODHIDHARMA

*Two monks were arguing about the temple flag.
One said the flag moved, the other said the
wind moved. Master Eno (638–713) overheard
them and said, "It is neither the wind nor the
flag, but your mind that moves." The monks
were speechless.*

We should take care not to make the intellect our god; it has, of course, powerful muscles, but no personality.

ALBERT EINSTEIN

Pure logic is the ruin of the spirit.

ANTOINE DE SAINT-EXUPÉRY

A mind all logic is like a knife all blade. It makes the hand bleed that uses it.

RABINDRANATH TAGORE

One of the things to come out of the home computer revolution could be the general and widespread understanding of how severely limited logic really is.

FRANK HERBERT

Computers are useless. They can only give you answers.

PABLO PICASSO

The way to solve the conflict between human values and technological needs is not to run away from technology. That's impossible. The way to resolve the conflict is to break down the barriers of dualistic thought that prevent a real understanding of what technology is—not an exploitation of nature, but a fusion of nature and the human spirit into a new kind of creation that transcends both.

ROBERT PIRSIG

We cannot get grace from gadgets.

J. B. PRIESTLEY

There is such a thing as subjective truth—the truth we make—negative on occasion, or positive, as the case may be. And this possesses far more power than do passive reflections of the factual world. Why not confess as much and begin living from the inside out? Why go on pretending to be "objective" or merely rational, when that is not our real nature at all? The natural thing for a human being is response and creation, not standing back.

ALEXANDER ELIOT

Since the concepts people live by are derived only from perceptions and from language and since perceptions are received and interpreted only in light of earlier concepts, man comes pretty close to living in a house that language built.

RUSSELL R. W. SMITH

Words, as is well known, are great foes
of reality.

JOSEPH CONRAD

Articulate words are a harsh clamor
and dissonance. When man arrives at
his highest perfection, he will again be
dumb!

NATHANIEL HAWTHORNE

Using words to describe magic is like
using a screwdriver to cut roast beef.

TOM ROBBINS

How describe the delicate thing that happens when a brilliant insect alights on a flower? Words, with their weight, fall upon the picture like birds of prey.

JULES RENARD

Having failed to distinguish thoughts from things, we then fail to distinguish words from thoughts. We think that if we can label a thing we have understood it.

MAHA STHAVIRA SANGHARAKSHITA

The map is not the territory.

ALFRED KORZBYBSKI

Truth is a river that is always splitting
up into two arms that reunite. Islanded
between the arms, the inhabitants argue
for a lifetime as to which is the main river.

CYRIL CONNOLLY

Our normal waking consciousness,
rational consciousness we call it, is but
one special type of consciousness, whilst
all about it, parted from it by the filmiest
of screens, there lie potential forms of
consciousness entirely different.

WILLIAM JAMES

The universe was a vast machine
yesterday, it is a hologram today. Who
knows what intellectual rattle we'll be
shaking tomorrow.

R. D. LAING

My studies in speculative philosophy,
metaphysics, and science are all summed
up in the image of a mouse called man
running in and out of every hole in the
cosmos hunting for the Absolute Cheese.

BENJAMIN DE CASSERES

What everyone has from his parents
innately is the Buddha Mind alone. But
since your parents themselves fail to
realize this, you become deluded too,
and then display this delusion in raising
your *own* children.

PETER HASKEL

In nature a repulsive caterpillar turns into a lovely butterfly. But with human beings it is the other way round: a lovely butterfly turns into a repulsive caterpillar.

ANTON CHEKHOV

A visitor arrived inquiring about Zen. Master Nan-in (1868–1912) silently poured him a cup of tea and continued pouring until the cup overflowed. "Why do you continue to pour after the cup is full?" asked the visitor. "To show you," replied Nan-in, "that you are like this cup: so full of your own preconceptions that nothing can go in. I can't tell you about Zen until you have emptied your cup."

From your first day at school you are cut
off from life to make theories.

TAISEN DESHIMARU

We are born princes and the civilizing
process makes us frogs.

ERIC BERNE

Our soul is cast into a body, where
it finds number, time, dimension.
Thereupon it reasons, and calls this
nature necessity, and can believe
nothing else.

LEWIS MUMFORD

Matter is less material and the mind
less spiritual than is generally supposed.
The habitual separation of physics
and psychology, mind and matter is
metaphysically indefensible.

BERTRAND RUSSELL

Man has such a predilection for systems
and abstract deductions that he is ready
to distort the truth intentionally, he is
ready to deny the evidence of his senses
only to justify his logic.

FYODOR DOSTOEVSKY

The concept, the label, is perpetually
hiding from us all the nature of the real.

JOYCE CARY

Rose is a rose is a rose is a rose.

GERTRUDE STEIN

Symbols are just symbols; the thing's the thing.

HOWARD OGDEN

Thinking doesn't seem to help very much. The human brain is too high-powered to have many practical uses in this particular universe.

KURT VONNEGUT

The world is too much with us; late and
  soon,
Getting and spending, we lay waste our
  powers:
Little we see in nature that is ours.
We have given our hearts away.

WILLIAM WORDSWORTH

To understand is almost the opposite of
existing.

GEORGES POULET

You are a principal work, a fragment of
God himself, you have in yourself part of
Him. Why then are you ignorant of your
high birth?

EPICTETUS

We do not err because truth is difficult to see. It is visible at a glance. We err because this is more comfortable.

ALEXANDR SOLZHENITSYN

Learn how to be entirely unreceptive to sensations arising from external forms, thereby purging your bodies of receptivity to externals.

HUANG PO

All that shimmers on the surface of the world, all that we call interesting, is the fruit of inebriation and ignorance.

E. M. CIORAN

At the bottom of the modern man there is always a great thirst for self-forgetfulness, self-distraction . . . and therefore he turns away from all those problems and abysses which might recall to him his own nothingness.

HENRI FRÉDÉRIC AMIEL

Many men go fishing all of their lives without knowing that it is not fish they are after.

HENRY DAVID THOREAU

How many times have you tried to shield yourself by reading the newspaper, watching television, or just spacing out? That is the $64,000 question: how much have you connected with yourself at all in your whole life?

CHÖGYAM TRUNGPA

Nobody today is normal, everybody is a little bit crazy or unbalanced, people's minds are running all the time. Their perceptions of the world are partial, incomplete. They are eaten alive by their egos. They think they see, but they are mistaken; all they do is project their madness, their world, upon the world. There is no clarity, no wisdom in that!

TAISEN DESHIMARU

Most of us have lost that sense of biosphere and humanity which would bind and reassure us all with an affirmation of beauty. Most of us do not today believe that whatever the ups and downs of detail within our limited experience, the larger whole is primarily beautiful.

GREGORY BATESON

All that we see or seem
Is but a dream within a dream.

EDGAR ALLAN POE

A man that is born falls into a dream like
a man who falls into the sea. If he tries
to climb out into the air as inexperienced
people endeavor to do, he drowns.

JOSEPH CONRAD

Beware lest you lose the substance by
grasping at the shadow.

AESOP

Physical concepts are free creations of the human mind, and are not, however it may seem, uniquely determined by the external world.

ALBERT EINSTEIN

No object is mysterious. The mystery is your eye.

ELIZABETH BOWEN

ATTACHMENT

Buddha's doctrine: man suffers because of his craving to possess and keep forever things which are essentially impermanent. Chief among these things is his own person, for this is his means of isolating himself from the rest of life, his castle into which he can retreat and from which he can assert himself against external forces. He believes that his fortified and isolated position is the best means of obtaining happiness; it enables him to fight against change, to strive to keep pleasing things for himself, to shut out suffering and shape circumstances as he wills. In short, it is his means of resisting life. The Buddha taught that all things, including his castle, are essentially impermanent and as soon as man tries to possess them they slip away; this frustration of the desire to possess is the immediate cause of suffering.

ALAN WATTS

Decent clothes . . . a car, but what's it all about?

MICHAEL CAINE
(IN *Alfie,* SCREENPLAY BY BILL NAUGHTON)

The love of money is the root of all evil.

Saint Paul

Our own soul, created wise and
thoughtful in the image of God, having
refused to know God, has become
bestial, senseless and almost insane
through delighting in material things.

Saint Gregory of Sinai

The feeling of satiety, almost inseparable
from large possessions, is a surer cause of
misery than ungratified desires.

Benjamin Disraeli

One clings to life although there is nothing to be called life; another clings to death although there is nothing to be called death. In reality there is nothing to be born, consequently, there is nothing to perish.

BODHIDHARMA

We can never have enough of that which we do not want.

ERIC HOFFER

Nothing very very good and nothing very very bad lasts for very very long.

DOUGLAS COUPLAND

Attachment is a manufacturer of illusion and whoever wants reality ought to be detached.

SIMONE WEIL

A young girl who became pregnant out of wedlock falsely identified Master Hakuin Ekaku (1685–1768) as the father. When the girl's parents confronted him, Hakuin said only, "Is that so?" When the child was born Hakuin cared for it lovingly as if it was his own until the girl finally admitted that she had lied. When the girl's parents apologized and begged his forgiveness, Hakuin replied, "Is that so?"

We grow weary of those things (and perhaps soonest) which we most desire.

SAMUEL BUTLER

Our desires always increase with our possessions. The knowledge that something remains yet unenjoyed impairs our enjoyment of the good before us.

SAMUEL JOHNSON

There must be more to life than having everything!

MAURICE SENDAK

If there is any peace it will come through being, not having.

HENRY MILLER

Man's many desires are like small metal coins he carries about in his pocket. The more he has the more they weigh him down.

SATYA SAI BABA

Complete possession is proved only by giving. All you are unable to give possesses you.

ANDRÉ GIDE

What you give is yours forever. What you keep is lost for all time.

OMAR SHARIF
(AS *Monsieur Ibrahim*, SCREENPLAY BY FRANCOIS DUPEYERON AND ERIC-EMMANUEL SCHMITT)

Possessions, outward success, publicity, luxury—to me these have always been contemptible. I believe that a simple and unassuming manner of life is best for everyone, best both for the body and the mind.

ALBERT EINSTEIN

We all want to be famous people, and the moment we want to *be* something we are no longer free.

JIDDU KRISHNAMURTI

I saw that nothing was permanent. You don't want to possess anything that is dear to you because you might lose it.

YOKO ONO

All worldly pursuits have but the one unavoidable and inevitable end, which is sorrow: acquisitions end in dispersion; buildings, in destruction; meetings, in separation; births, in death. Knowing this, one should, from the very first, renounce acquisition and heaping up, and building, and meeting; and, faithful to the commands of an eminent guru, set about realizing the Truth.

MILAREPA

SELF

What is the way of the Buddha? It is to study the self. What is the study of the self? It is to forget oneself. To forget oneself is to be enlightened by everything in the world.

DOGEN

The urge to transcend self-conscious selfhood is a principal appetite of the soul.

ALDOUS HUXLEY

The true value of a human being is determined primarily by the measure and sense in which he has attained liberation from the self.

ALBERT EINSTEIN

Until we lose ourselves there is no hope of finding ourselves.

HENRY MILLER

Master Bankei (1622–1693) was eulogized
by a blind man: "Since I cannot see a person's
face, I must judge his sincerity by his voice.
Usually when I hear someone congratulate
a friend on some success, I also hear envy
in his voice, and when I hear expressions of
condolence, I hear a secret tone of pleasure.
Not so with Bankei; when he expressed
happiness, his voice was completely happy,
and when he expressed sadness, sadness was
all I heard."

The more a human being feels himself a
self, tries to intensify this self and reach
a never attainable perfection, the more
drastically he steps out of the center of
being, which is no longer now his own
center, and the further he removes
himself from it.

EUGEN HERRIGEL

Self is the root, the tree, and the branches of all the evils of our fallen state.

WILLIAM LAW

Forgetfulness of self is remembrance of God.

BAYAZID AL-BISTAMI

The search "Who am I" . . . ends in the annihilation of the illusory "I" and the Self which remains over will be as clear as a gooseberry in the palm of one's hand.

SRI RAMANA MAHARSHI

The mastery of nature is vainly believed to be an adequate substitute for self-mastery.

REINHOLD NIEBUHR

There's only one corner of the universe you can be certain of improving and that's your own self.

ALDOUS HUXLEY

It is better to conquer yourself than to win a thousand battles. Then the victory is yours. It cannot be taken from you, not by angels or by demons, heaven or hell.

THE BUDDHA

To reach perfection, we must all pass, one by one, through the death of self-effacement.

DAG HAMMARSKJÖLD

Nothing burns in hell but the self.

Theologica Germanica

Trying to define yourself is like trying to bite your own teeth.

ALAN WATTS

TIME

Time is not a line, but a series of now-points.

TAISEN DESHIMARU

In order to be utterly happy the only thing necessary is to refrain from comparing this moment with other moments in the past, which I often did not fully enjoy because I was comparing them with other moments of the future.

ANDRÉ GIDE

The present moment is a powerful goddess.

JOHANN WOLFGANG VON GOETHE

There's no present. There's only the immediate future and the recent past.

GEORGE CARLIN

The most important thing I learned on Tralfamadore was that when a person dies he only *appears* to die. He

is still very much alive in the past, so
it is very silly for people to cry at his
funeral. All moments, past, present, and
future, always have existed, always will
exist. The Tralfamadorians can look at
all the different moments just the way
we can look at a stretch of the Rocky
Mountains, for instance. They can see
how permanent all the moments are,
and they can look at any moment that
interests them. It is just an illusion that
we have here on Earth that one moment
follows another one, like beads on a
string, and that once a moment is gone it
is gone forever.

KURT VONNEGUT

There is no present or future, only the
past, happening over and over again, now.

EUGENE O'NEILL

We cannot put off living until we are ready. The most salient characteristic of life is its coerciveness: it is always urgent, "here and now" without any possible postponement. Life is fired at us point blank.

José Ortega y Gasset

No mind is much employed upon the present; recollection and anticipation fill up almost all our moments.

Samuel Johnson

The word "now" is like a bomb through the window, and it ticks.

Arthur Miller

Tom Seaver: *Hey, Yogi, what time is it?*
Yogi Berra: *You mean now?*

The passing moment is all that we can be sure of; it is only common sense to extract its utmost value from it; the future will one day be the present and will seem as unimportant as the present does now.

W. SOMERSET MAUGHAM

Time and space are fragments of the infinite for the use of finite creatures.

HENRI FRÉDÉRIC AMIEL

Time is the longest distance between two places.

TENNESSEE WILLIAMS

Time is the only true purgatory.

Samuel Butler

I am in the present. I cannot know what tomorrow will bring forth. I can know only what the truth is for me today. That is what I am called upon to serve, and I serve it in all lucidity.

Igor Stravinsky

Take therefore no thought for the morrow: for the morrow shall take thought for the things of itself. Sufficient unto the day is the evil thereof.

Matthew 6:34

Tomorrow's life is too late. Live today.

Martial

Life is all memory except for the one present moment that goes by so quick you can hardly catch it going.

TENNESSEE WILLIAMS

What then is time? If no one asks me, I know what it is. If I wish to explain it to him who asks, I do not know.

SAINT AUGUSTINE

Time is but the stream I go a-fishing in.

HENRY DAVID THOREAU

Only our concept of Time makes it possible for us to speak of the Day of Judgment by that name; in reality it is a summary court in perpetual session.

FRANZ KAFKA

I have realized that the past and the future are real illusions, that they exist only in the present, which is what there is and all that there is.

ALAN WATTS

To realize the unimportance of time is the gate of wisdom.

BERTRAND RUSSELL

We can never finally know. I simply believe that some part of the human Self or Soul is not subject to the laws of space and time.

CARL JUNG

LIFE

Life is suffering.

THE BUDDHA

Life just is. You have to flow with it.
Give yourself to the moment. Let it
happen.

JERRY BROWN

If it were possible to talk to the unborn,
one could never explain to them how it
feels to be alive, for life is washed in the
speechless real.

JACQUES BARZUN

We are involved in a life that passes
understanding and our highest business
is our daily life.

JOHN CAGE

Life is a child playing around your feet,
a tool you hold firmly in your grip, a
bench you sit down upon in the evening,
in your garden.

JEAN ANOUILH

Life eludes logic.

ANDRÉ GIDE

No concept is a carrier of life.

CARL JUNG

Life happens too fast for you to ever think about it. If you could just persuade people of this, but they insist on amassing information.

KURT VONNEGUT

The best way to prepare for life is to begin to live.

ELBERT HUBBARD

Life is not a problem to be solved but a reality to be experienced.

SOREN KIERKEGAARD

If there is a sin against life, it consists perhaps not so much in despairing of life as in hoping for another life and in eluding the implacable grandeur of this life.

Albert Camus

There is no end. There is no beginning. There is only the infinite passion of life.

Federico Fellini

There is no cure for birth and death, save to enjoy the interval.

George Santayana

What a miserable thing life is: you're living in clover, only the clover isn't good enough.

BERTOLT BRECHT

Great minds struggle to cure diseases so that people may live longer, but only madmen ask why. One lives longer in order that he may live longer. There is no other purpose.

ROBERT PIRSIG

Dreams are real while they last. Can we say more of life?

HAVELOCK ELLIS

DEATH

Die in your thoughts every morning and you will no longer fear death.

HAGAKURE

A dying man needs to die as a sleepy man needs to sleep, and there comes a time when it is wrong, as well as useless, to resist.

STEWART ALSOP

The Buddhist Sutra of Mindfulness speaks about the meditation on the corpse: meditate on the decomposition of the body, how the body bloats and turns violet, how it is eaten by worms until only bits of blood and flesh still cling to the bones, meditate up to the

point where only white bones remain,
which in turn are slowly worn away
and turn into dust. Meditate like that,
knowing that your own body will
undergo the same process. Meditate
on the corpse until you are calm and at
peace, until your mind and heart are
light and tranquil and a smile appears on
your face. Thus, by overcoming revulsion
and fear, life will be seen as infinitely
precious, every second of it worth living.

THICH NHAT HANH

Birth is not one act; it is a process. The
aim of life is to be fully born, though its
tragedy is that most of us die before we
are thus born. To live is to be born every
minute. Death occurs when birth stops.

ERICH FROMM

It is told that Buddha, going out to look
on life, was greatly daunted by death.
"They all eat one another!" he cried, and
called it evil. This process I examined,
changed the verb, said, "They all feed
one another," and called it good.

CHARLOTTE PERKINS GILMAN

Look! Look! If you look really hard at
things you'll forget you're going to die.

MONTGOMERY CLIFT

While alive
Be a dead man,
Thoroughly dead;
And act as you will,
And all is good.

BUNAN

Those who cling to life die, and those who defy death live.

UYESUGI KENSHIN

I postpone death by living, by suffering, by error, by risking, by giving, by losing.

ANAÏS NIN

The world is impermanent. One should constantly remember death.

SRI RAMAKRISHNA

While I thought I was learning how to live, I have been learning how to die.

LEONARDO DA VINCI

It takes so many years
To learn that one is dead.

T. S. Eliot

Human beings are afraid of dying. They
are always running after something:
money, honor, pleasure. But if you had to
die now, what would you want?

Taisen Deshimaru

We die, and we do not die.

Shunryu Suzuki

REALITY

Observe things as they are and don't pay
attention to other people.

Huang Po

We have no right to assume that any physical laws exist, or if they have existed up to now, that they will continue to exist in a similar manner in the future.

MAX PLANCK

There is no reality except the one contained within us. That is why so many people live such an unreal life. They take the images outside them for reality and never allow the world within to assert itself.

HERMAN HESSE

Reality is where we are from moment to moment.

ROBERT LINSSEN

Reality is a staircase going neither up or down. We don't move, today is today, always is today.

OCTAVIO PAZ

Any intellectually conceived object is *always* in the past and therefore *unreal.* Reality is always the moment of vision *before* the intellectualization takes place. *There is no other reality.*

ROBERT PIRSIG

What we call reality is an agreement that people have arrived at to make life more livable.

LOUISE NEVELSON

Reality has no inside, outside, or middle part.

Bodhidharma

Humankind
Cannot bear very much reality.

T. S. Eliot

We take our shape, it is true, within and
against that cage of reality bequeathed
to us at our birth; and yet it is precisely
through our dependence on this reality
that we are most endlessly betrayed.

James Baldwin

The man bent over his guitar,
A shearsman of sorts. The day was green.
They said, "You have a blue guitar,

You do not play things as they are."
The man replied, "Things as they are
Are changed upon a blue guitar."

WALLACE STEVENS

An independent reality in the ordinary
physical sense can neither be ascribed to
the phenomenon nor to the agencies of
observation.

NIELS BOHR

As far as the laws of mathematics refer
to reality, they are not certain; as far as
they are certain, they do not refer to
reality.

ALBERT EINSTEIN

Reality is not clearly and immediately apprehended, except by those who have made themselves loving, pure in heart and poor in spirit.

ALDOUS HUXLEY

The ancient intuition that all matter, all "reality," is energy, that all phenomena, including time and space, are mere crystallizations of mind, is an idea with which few physicists have quarreled since the theory of relativity first called into question the separate identities of energy and matter. Today most scientists would agree with the ancient Hindus that nothing exists or is destroyed, things merely change shape or form; that matter is insubstantial in origin, a temporary aggregate of the pervasive energy that animates the electron.

PETER MATTHIESSEN

I like reality. It tastes of bread.

JEAN ANOUILH

There is no way you can use the
word "reality" without quotation marks
around it.

JOSEPH CAMPBELL

We should tackle reality in a slightly
jokey way, otherwise we miss its point.

LAWRENCE DURRELL

Everything factual is, in a sense, theory. The blue of the sky exhibits the basic laws of chromatics. There is no sense in looking for something behind phenomena: they *are* theory.

JOHANN WOLFGANG VON GOETHE

Any experience of reality is indescribable!

R. D. LAING

Cloquet hated reality but realized it was still the only place to get a good steak.

WOODY ALLEN

ENLIGHTENMENT

NATURE

Hope and fear cannot change the seasons.

CHÖGYAM TRUNGPA

Nature is what she is—amoral and persistent.

STEPHEN JAY GOULD

Nature is not anthropomorphic.

LAO TZU

Wind moving through grass so that the grass quivers. This moves me with an emotion I don't even understand.

KATHERINE MANSFIELD

Handle even a single leaf of green in such a way that it manifests the body of the Buddha. This in turn allows the Buddha to manifest through the leaf.

DOGEN

Except during the nine months before he draws his first breath, no man manages his affairs as well as a tree does.

GEORGE BERNARD SHAW

It's very nice to feel. You're nothing. You're just nothing when you're near a volcano.

KATIA KRAFFT

Every individual is an expression of the whole realm of nature, a unique action of the total universe.

ALAN WATTS

No snowflake falls in an inappropriate place.

ZEN MAXIM

There is nothing useless in nature; not even uselessness itself.

MICHEL DE MONTAIGNE

Nature hath no goal though she hath law.

JOHN DONNE

Nature has neither kernel nor shell; she is everything at once.

JOHANN WOLFGANG VON GOETHE

Whether you like it or not, whether you know it or not, secretly all nature seeks God and works toward him.

MEISTER ECKHART

I believe in God, only I spell it Nature.

FRANK LLOYD WRIGHT

The world is *not* to be put in order, the world *is* order incarnate. It is for us to put ourselves in unison with this order.

HENRY MILLER

To the dull mind nature is leaden. To the illumined mind the whole world burns and sparkles with light.

RALPH WALDO EMERSON

My father considered a walk among the mountains as the equivalent of churchgoing.

ALDOUS HUXLEY

Ink cannot tell the glow that lights me this moment in turning to the mountains. I feel strong [enough] to leap Yosemite walls at a bound.

JOHN MUIR

Monk: *"Where can I enter Zen?"*
Master Gensha *(831–908): "Can you hear the babbling brook?"*
Monk: *"Yes, I can hear it."*
Gensha: *"Then enter there."*

The clearest way into the universe is through a forest wilderness.

JOHN MUIR

There is something about the Himalayas not possessed by the Alps, something unseen and unknown, a charm that pervades every hour spent among them, a mystery intriguing and disturbing. Confronted by them, a man loses his grasp of ordinary things, perceiving

himself as immortal, an entity capable
of outdistancing all change, all decay, all
life, all death.

FRANK SMYTHE

What I know of the divine science and
Holy Scripture I learnt in woods and
fields.

SAINT BERNARD

Speak to the earth, and it shall teach
thee.

JOB 12:8

Earth, with her thousand voices, praises
God.

SAMUEL TAYLOR COLERIDGE

The world is charged with the grandeur of God.

GERARD MANLEY HOPKINS

It were happy if we studied nature more in natural things, and acted according to nature, whose rules are few, plain, and most reasonable.

WILLIAM PENN

The violets in the mountains have broken the rocks.

TENNESSEE WILLIAMS

There is nothing that is supernatural, however mysterious, in the whole system of our redemption; every part of it has its ground in the workings and powers

of nature and all our redemption is only
nature set right, or made to be that
which it ought to be.

William Law

Years ago, after I first started to make
a bit of money, I used to go to the local
garden center every fall and purchase
fifty-two daffodil bulbs. Shortly
thereafter, I would go to my parents'
backyard with a deck of fifty-two wax
coated playing cards and hurl the cards
across the lawn. Wherever a card
fell, I would plant one of the bulbs. Of
course, I could have just tossed the bulbs
themselves, but the point of the matter is,
I *didn't*.

Planting bulbs this way creates a very
natural spray effect—the same silent
algorithms that dictate the torque in a
flock of sparrows or the gnarl of a piece

of driftwood also dictate success in this formal matter, too.

And come spring, after the daffodils and narcissi have spoken their delicate little haikus to the world and spilled their cold, gentle scent, their crinkly beige onion paper remnants inform us that summer will soon be here and that it is now time to mow the lawn.

DOUGLAS COUPLAND

An old pond—
The sound of the water
When a frog jumps in.

BASHO

THE WAY

Those who seek the truth by means of intellect and learning only get further and further away from it. Not till your thoughts cease all their branching here and there, not till you abandon all thoughts of seeking for something, not till your mind is motionless as wood or stone, will you be on the right road to the Gate.

HUANG PO

I searched through rebellion, drugs, diets, mysticism, religions, intellectualism, and much more, only to find . . . that truth is basically simple— and feels good, clean and right.

CHICK COREA

All composite things decay; work out your salvation with diligence.

THE BUDDHA

You must make the most strenuous efforts. Throughout this life, you can never be certain of living long enough to take another breath.

HUANG PO

It does not matter how slowly you go so long as you do not stop.

CONFUCIUS

You don't have to try, you just have to be.

DAVID VISCOTT

All know the way; few actually walk it.

BODHIDHARMA

When a monk asked, "What is the Tao?"
Master Ummon (863–949) replied, "Walk on."

If you follow the present-day world, you will turn your back on the Way; if you would not turn your back on the Way, do not follow the world.

TAKUAN

There is a goal but no way; what we call the way is mere wavering.

FRANZ KAFKA

The truth knocks on the door and you
say, "Go away, I'm looking for the truth,"
and so it goes away. Puzzling.

ROBERT PIRSIG

Believe those who are seeking the truth;
doubt those who find it.

ANDRÉ GIDE

Mumonkan *(The Gateless Gate):*
A collection of forty-eight koan *compiled by
the Zen monk Mumon Ekai (1183–1260). Its
title derives from the verse:*
> *The great path has no gates,*
> *Thousands of roads enter it.*
> *When one passes through this gateless gate*
> *He walks freely between heaven and earth.*

If a man wants to be of the greatest possible value to his fellow-creatures, let him begin the long, solitary task of perfecting himself.

ROBERTSON DAVIES

Do not seek to follow in the footsteps of the men of old; seek what they sought.

BASHO

The true way goes over a rope which is not stretched at any great height but just above the ground. It seems more designed to make men stumble than to be walked upon.

FRANZ KAFKA

If a man wishes to be sure of the road
he treads on, he must close his eyes and
walk in the dark.

SAINT JOHN OF THE CROSS

To have his path made clear for him is the
aspiration of every human being in our
beclouded and tempestuous existence.

JOSEPH CONRAD

Experience, which destroys innocence,
also leads one back to it.

JAMES BALDWIN

First there is a time when we believe
everything without reasons, then
for a little while we believe with
discrimination, then we believe nothing

whatever, and then we believe everything again—and, moreover, give reasons why we believe everything.

G. C. LICHTENBERG

The course of every intellectual, if he pursues his journey long and unflinchingly enough, ends in the obvious, from which the nonintellectuals have never stirred.

ALDOUS HUXLEY

The Perfect Way is only difficult for those who pick and choose; do not like, do not dislike; all will then be clear. Make a hairbreadth difference, and Heaven and Earth are set apart.

SENG TS'AN

To be surprised, to wonder, is to begin
to understand.

José Ortega y Gasset

I wonder why. I wonder why.
I wonder why I wonder.
I wonder *why* I wonder why
I wonder why I wonder!

Richard P. Feynman

To attain Buddhahood . . . we must
scatter this life's aims and objects to the
wind.

Milarepa

The Way that can be told is not the
eternal way.

Lao Tzu

People of this world are deluded. They're always longing for something, always, in a word, seeking. But the wise wake up. They choose reason over custom. They fix their minds on the sublime and let their bodies change with the seasons.

BODHIDHARMA

When you seek it, you cannot find it.

ZEN MAXIM

Not only has one to do one's best, one must, while doing one's best, remain detached from whatever one is trying to achieve.

JANWILLEM VAN DE WETERING

If you know that fundamentally there is nothing to seek, you have settled your affairs.

RINZAI

The bird of paradise alights only upon the hand that does not grasp.

JOHN BERRY

If thou shouldst say, "It is enough, I have reached perfection," all is lost. For it is the function of perfection to make one know one's imperfection.

SAINT AUGUSTINE

Every day Master Shigen (c. 900) had the
following dialogue with himself:
　"Hey, Master!"
　"Yes?"
　"Are you listening?"
　"Yes."
　"Don't be complacent!"
　"I won't!"

I had been proud of my awareness, aware
of my pride, and proud of that awareness
again. It went on like this: how clever
I am that I know I am so stupid, how
stupid I am to think that I am so clever,
and how clever I am that I am aware of
my stupidity, etc.

JANWILLEM VAN DE WETERING

Attachment to spiritual things is . . . just as much an attachment as inordinate love of anything else.

THOMAS MERTON

What is important . . . is not the right doctrine but the attainment of the true experience. It is giving up believing in belief.

ALAN KEIGHTLEY

The problem is that ego can convert anything to its own use, even spirituality. Ego is constantly attempting to acquire and apply the teachings of spirituality for its own benefit.

CHÖGYAM TRUNGPA

The search for happiness is one of the chief sources of unhappiness.

ERIC HOFFER

When a monk asked, "What is the Buddha?" Ummon (863–949) replied, "A shit-wiping stick."

A person who says, "I'm enlightened" probably isn't.

BABA RAM DASS

The Zen expression "Kill the Buddha!" means to kill any concept of the Buddha as something apart from oneself. To kill the Buddha is to *be* the Buddha.

PETER MATTHIESSEN

Look. This is your world! You can't not
look. There is no other world. This is
your world; it is your feast. You inherited
this; you inherited these eyeballs; you
inherited this world of color. Look at
the greatness of the whole thing. Look!
Don't hesitate—look! Open your eyes.
Don't blink, and look, look—look
further.

CHÖGYAM TRUNGPA

There is no need to run outside
For better seeing, . . .
 . . . Rather abide
At the center of your being;
For the more you leave it, the less you
    learn.
Search your heart and see
 . . .
The way is to be.

LAO TZU

NO-KNOWLEDGE

I do not understand Buddhism.

Hui Neng

Knowledge is knowing as little as possible.

Charles Bukowski

To know what we do not know is the beginning of wisdom.

Maha Sthavira Sangharakshita

To know that you do not know is the best. To pretend to know when you do not know is a disease.

Lao Tzu

Sometimes it proves the highest
understanding not to understand.

BALTASAR GRACIÁN

Opinions breed anger, nourish hate,
ossify the heart, narrow the mind.

SEAN O'FAOLAIN

What shall I say about poetry? What shall
I say about those clouds, or about the
sky? Look; look at them; look at it! And
nothing more. Don't you understand that
a poet can't say anything about poetry?
Leave that to the critics and professors.
For neither you, nor I, nor any poet
knows what poetry is.

FEDERICO GARCÍA LORCA

All I know about method is that when
I am not working I sometimes think
I know something, but when I am
working, it is quite clear I know nothing.

JOHN CAGE

I don't know. I don't care. And it doesn't
make any difference.

JACK KEROUAC

What is the truth? I don't know and I'm
sorry I brought it up.

EDWARD ABBEY

All that we know is nothing, we are merely crammed wastepaper baskets, unless we are in touch with that which laughs at all our knowing.

D. H. LAWRENCE

Nothing is more conducive to peace of mind than not having any opinion at all.

G. C. LICHTENBERG

I know nothing except the fact of my ignorance.

SOCRATES

Interviewer: *"I've got lots of questions to ask you, Yogi."*
Yogi Berra: *"If you ask me anything I don't know, I'm not going to answer."*

He who knows does not speak;
He who speaks does not know.

Lao Tzu

I lead up and down, across, and to and
fro my pupils by the nose—and learn
that we in truth can nothing know.

Johann Wolfgang von Goethe

How dieth the wise man? As the fool.

Ecclesiastes 2:16

As we acquire more knowledge, things
do not become more comprehensible,
but more mysterious.

Will Durant

All affirmations are true in some sense,
false in some sense, meaningless in some
sense, true and false in some sense, true
and meaningless in some sense, and true
and false and meaningless in some sense.

SRI SYADASTI

We are here and it is now. Further than
that all human knowledge is moonshine.

H. L. MENCKEN

Imagination is more important than
knowledge.

ALBERT EINSTEIN

We know too much and feel too little.

BERTRAND RUSSELL

It is the tragedy of the world that no one knows what he doesn't know; and the less a man knows, the more sure he is that he knows everything.

JOYCE CARY

Reports that say that something hasn't happened are always interesting to me, because as we know, there are known knowns; there are things we know we know. We also know there are known unknowns; that is to say we know there are some things we do not know. But there are also unknown unknowns—the ones we don't know we don't know.

DONALD RUMSFELD

One of the functions of intelligence is to take account of the dangers that come from trusting solely to the intelligence.

Lewis Mumford

Intelligence is silence, truth being invisible. But what a racket I make declaring this.

Ned Rorem

Whereof one cannot speak, thereof one must be silent.

Ludwig Wittgenstein

Don't believe everything you think.

Anonymous

There are more things in heaven and
earth, Horatio,
Than are dreamt of in your philosophy.

WILLIAM SHAKESPEARE (Hamlet)

One never knows, do one?

FATS WALLER

In baseball, you don't know *nothing*.

YOGI BERRA

MEDITATION

Men cannot see their reflection in running water, but only in still water.

CHUANG TZU

What is called zazen is sitting on a *zafu* [pillow] in a quiet room, absolutely still, in the exact and proper position and without uttering a word, the mind empty of any thought, good or wicked. It is continuing to sit peacefully, facing a wall, and nothing more. Every day.

TAISEN DESHIMARU

Man's great misfortune is that he has
no organ, no kind of eyelid or brake, to
mask or block a thought, or all thought,
when he wants to.

PAUL VALÉRY

In doing zazen it is desirable to have a
quiet room. You should be temperate
in eating and drinking, forsaking all
delusive relationships. Setting everything
aside, think of neither good nor evil,
right nor wrong. Thus having stopped
the various functions of your mind, give
up even the idea of becoming a Buddha.

DOGEN

Zazen *is seated meditation—the opposite of
contemplation—the emptying of the mind of
all thoughts in order simply* to be.

In the midst of all good and evil, not a thought is aroused in the mind—this is called *za*. Seeing into one's Self-nature, not being moved at all—this is called *zen*.

Hui Neng

Zazen is not the practice of self-improvement, like a course in making friends and influencing people. With earnest zazen, character change does occur, but this is not a matter of ego-adjustment. It is forgetting the self.

Robert Aitken

For the ordinary man, whose mind is a checkerboard of crisscrossing reflections, opinions, and prejudices, bare attention is virtually impossible; his life is thus centered not in reality itself but in his *ideas* of it. By focusing the mind wholly

on each object and every action, zazen
strips it of extraneous thoughts and
allows us to enter into a full rapport
with life.

Philip Kapleau

Sitting is the gateway of truth to total
liberation.

Dogen

During zazen, brain and consciousness
become pure. It's exactly like muddy
water left to stand in a glass. Little by
little, the sediment sinks to the bottom
and the water becomes pure.

Taisen Deshimaru

Meditation is not a means to an end. It is both the means and the end.

Jiddu Krishnamurti

Zazen itself is God.

Dogen

Teach us to care and not to care
Teach us to sit still.

T. S. Eliot

We are sick with fascination for the useful tools of names and numbers, of symbols, signs, conceptions and ideas. Meditation is therefore the art of suspending verbal and symbolic thinking

for a time, somewhat as a courteous
audience will stop talking when a
concert is about to begin.

ALAN WATTS

No thought, no action, no movement,
total stillness: only thus can one manifest
the true nature and law of things from
within and unconsciously, and at last
become one with heaven and earth.

LAO TZU

You do not need to leave your room.
Remain sitting at your table and listen.
Do not even listen, simply wait. Do not
even wait, be quite still and solitary. The
world will freely offer itself to you to be
unmasked, it has no choice, it will roll in
ecstasy at your feet.

FRANZ KAFKA

In zazen, one is one's present self,
what one was, and what one will be,
all at once.

PETER MATTHIESSEN

When one devotes oneself to meditation,
mental burdens, unnecessary worries,
and wandering thoughts drop off one
by one; life seems to run smoothly and
pleasantly. A student may now depend
on intuition to make decisions. As one
acts on intuition, second thought, with
its dualism, doubt and hesitation, does
not arise.

NYOGEN SENZAKI

If you have a glass full of liquid you can
discourse forever on its qualities, discuss
whether it is cold, warm, whether it

is really and truly composed of H_2O,
or mineral water, or saki. *Zazen is
drinking it.*

TAISEN DESHIMARU

The uniqueness of zazen lies in this:
that the mind is freed from bondage to
all thought forms, visions, objects, and
imaginings, however sacred or elevating,
and brought to a state of absolute
emptiness, from which alone it may one
day perceive its own true nature, or the
nature of the universe.

PHILIP KAPLEAU

All the masters tell us that the reality
of life—which our noisy waking
consciousness prevents us from
hearing—speaks to us chiefly in silence.

KARLFRIED GRAF DÜRCKHEIM

I neglect God and his angels for the noise of a fly, for the rattling of a coach, for the whining of a door.

JOHN DONNE

People dread zazen like a desert trip. It seems to be dead, dry, empty. But if they sit long enough and dig deep enough they find everything is right after all. There is water in the desert.

SONG RYONG HEARN

The quieter you become the more you can hear.

BABA RAM DASS

If zazen were all that was needed to attain Satori, then frogs would be Buddhas.

ZEN MAXIM

All religions will pass, but this will remain: simply sitting in a chair and looking in the distance.

V. V. ROZANOV

SATORI

Wonder of wonders! Intrinsically all living beings are Buddhas, endowed with wisdom and virtue, but because men's minds have become inverted through delusive thinking they fail to perceive this.

THE BUDDHA

It was a morning in early summer. A silver haze shimmered and trembled over the lime trees. The air was laden with their fragrance. The temperature was like a caress. I remember—I need not recall—that I climbed up a tree stump and felt suddenly immersed in Itness. I did not call it by that name. I had no need for words. It and I were one.

BERNARD BERENSON

It is in the unearthly first hour of twilight that earth's almost agonized livingness is felt. This hour is so dreadful to some people that they hurry indoors to turn on the lights.

ELIZABETH BOWEN

The interface between bliss and madness
is as thin as the skin of an eyeball.

ALEXANDER ELIOT

Essentially Satori is a sudden experience,
and it is often described as a "turning
over" of the mind, just as a pair of scales
will suddenly turn over when a sufficient
amount of material has been poured
into one pan to overbalance the weight
in the other. Hence it is an experience
which generally occurs after a long and
concentrated effort to discover the
meaning of Zen.

ALAN WATTS

I entered (into my inward self) and
beheld with the eye of my soul . . . the
Light Unchangeable.

SAINT AUGUSTINE

At midnight I abruptly awakened. At first my mind was foggy. . . . Then all at once I was struck as though by lightning, and the next instant heaven and earth crumbled and disappeared. Instantaneously, like surging waves, a tremendous delight welled up in me, a veritable hurricane of delight, as I laughed wildly and loudly, "There's no reasoning here, no reasoning at all! Ha! Ha! Ha!" The empty sky split in two, then opened its enormous mouth and began to laugh uproariously: "Ha! Ha! Ha!"

KOUN YAMADA

I sat there listening with my whole being, and with my whole strength contemplating that mountain that I so dearly love. . . . Was there anyone in the world, at that moment, as happy as I?

COLETTE RICHARD

At the next meal—I was head server—
tears were pouring down my face as
I served . . . and afterwards, when I
went out of the *zendo* . . . there was a
tree there, and looking at the tree, I
didn't feel I was the tree, it went deeper
than that. I felt the wind on me, I felt
the birds on me, all separation was
completely gone.

BERNARD TETSUGEN GLASSMAN

I was not looking now at an unusual
flower arrangement. I was seeing what
Adam had seen on the morning of his
creation—the miracle, moment by
moment, of naked existence.

ALDOUS HUXLEY

Buddha-nature: *The intrinsic perfection of
all living beings that Zen seeks to realize.*

You are sitting on the earth and you realize that this earth deserves you and you deserve this earth. You are there—fully, personally, genuinely.

CHÖGYAM TRUNGPA

Suddenly I was ruined and homeless.

JOSHU

I was sitting by the ocean one late summer afternoon, watching the waves rolling in and feeling the rhythm of my breathing, when suddenly I became aware of my whole environment as being engaged in a gigantic cosmic dance. . . . I "saw" cascades of energy coming down from outer space, in which particles were created and destroyed in rhythmic pulses; I "saw" the atoms of those elements and those of my body participating in this cosmic dance of energy; I felt its rhythm and I "heard" its sound, and at that moment I *knew* that this was the Dance of Shiva, the Lord of Dancers worshiped by the Hindus.

FRITJOF CAPRA

I took a walk. Suddenly I stood still, filled with the realization that I had no body or mind. All I could see was one great illuminating Whole—omnipresent, perfect, lucid and serene.

HAN SHAN

I suddenly felt very happy . . . I felt about me a steadily rising tide of enormous joy. . . . The warmth of the tide was glorious, as of a huge, affectionate flame. I remained intellectually conscious; that is, I was critical of my own condition,

considering it, comparing it, wondering
what it might mean. Never before had I
attained this discriminate consciousness
which functions on a plane where all
discrimination seemed absurd. Then
the tide ebbed slowly and I was left
exhilarated, rested, refreshed.

CHRISTMAS HUMPHREYS

If the doors of perception were cleansed
every thing would appear to man as it is,
infinite.

WILLIAM BLAKE

This moment, this being, is the thing.
My life is all life in little. The moon, the
planets, pass around my heart. The sun,
now hidden by the round bulk of this
earth, shines into me, and in me as well.
The gods and the angels both good and

bad are like the hairs of my own head, seemingly numberless, and growing from within. I people the cosmos from myself, it seems, yet what am I? A puff of dust, or a brief coughing spell, with emptiness and silence to follow.

ALEXANDER ELIOT

Kwatz!: *An exclamation used by Zen masters to shock a student out of dualistic thinking.*

Zen masters hold that an individual's full understanding of Zen is often precipitated by the hearing of a single phrase exactly calculated to destroy his particular demon of ignorance; so they have always favored the brief paradoxical dialogue as a means of instruction, finding it of great value in giving a sudden jolt to a pupil's mind which may propel him towards or over the brink of Enlightenment.

JOHN BLOFELD

Philosophy lives in words, but truth and fact well up into our lives in ways that exceed verbal formulation. There is in the living act of perception always something that glimmers and twinkles and will not be caught, and for which reflection comes too late.

WILLIAM JAMES

Knowing others is wisdom, knowing yourself is enlightenment.

LAO TZU

Any enlightenment which requires to
be authenticated, certified, recognized,
congratulated, is (as yet) a false, or at
least incomplete one.

R. H. BLYTH

This is It
and I am It
and You are It
and so is That
and He is It
and She is It
And It is It
And That is That.

JAMES BROUGHTON

The universe begins to look more like a
great thought than a great machine.

SIR JAMES JEANS

That the world is, is the mystical.

LUDWIG WITTGENSTEIN

Penetrating so many secrets, we cease to believe in the unknowable. But there it sits nevertheless, calmly licking its chops.

H. L. MENCKEN

We carry within us the wonders we seek without us.

SIR THOMAS BROWNE

The kingdom of God is within you.

LUKE 17:21

To obtain satori, one must let go of the ego. To receive everything, one must open one's hands and give.

TAISEN DESHIMARU

You can't be lonely on the sea—you're too alone.

TANIA AEBI

A simple fishing boat in the midst of the rippling waters is enough to awaken in the mind of the beholder a sense of the vastness of the sea and at the same time of peace and contentment—the Zen sense of the alone.

D. T. SUZUKI

The aim of Zen training is to attain the state of consciousness which occurs when the individual ego is emptied of itself and becomes identified with the infinite reality of all things.

ANNE BANCROFT

After many years of work on the koan Mu, *Mumon Ekai (1183–1260) had a Great Awakening when he heard the dinner drum. When asked to describe his satori he said, "It would be easier for a mule to explain his dreams."*

All the problems vanish when you are in the nonverbal dimension of consciousness. Theology, philosophy and metaphysics as we ordinarily talk about them cease to be urgent problems. You see the answers to all the questions that theologians and metaphysicians ask and you see why their questions are absurd.

LUDWIG WITTGENSTEIN

It is inner abandonment that leads men to the highest truth.

HENRY SUSO

When, in its [the soul's] divine power, it completely possesses the body, it converts that into a luminous moving cloud and thus can manifest itself in the whole of its divinity. This is the explanation of the miracle of St. Francis walking on the sea. His body no longer weighed like ours, so light had it become through the soul.

ISADORA DUNCAN

The one and only thing required is to free oneself from the bondage of mind and body alike, putting the Buddha's own seal upon yourself. If you do this as you sit in ecstatic meditation, the whole universe itself scattered through the infinity of space turns into enlightenment. That is what I mean by the Buddha's seal.

DOGEN

If we achieve satori and the satori shows, like a bit of dogshit stuck on the tip of our nose, that is not so good.

TAISEN DESHIMARU

When reality is perceived in its nature of ultimate perfection, the practitioner has reached a level of wisdom called non-discrimination mind—a wondrous communion in which there is no longer any distinction made between subject and object.

THICH NHAT HAHN

MIND

BEGINNER'S MIND

If your mind is empty, it is always ready
for anything; it is open to everything.
In the beginner's mind there are many
possibilities, but in the expert's there
are few.

SHUNRYU SUZUKI

When you're green, you're growing.
When you're ripe, you rot.

RAY KROC

To understand truth one must have a very
sharp, precise, clear mind; not a cunning
mind, but a mind that is capable of
looking without any distortion, a mind
innocent and vulnerable.

JIDDU KRISHNAMURTI

Consciousness is always open to many possibilities because it involves play. It is always an adventure.

JULIAN JAYNES

It is better to ask some of the questions than to know all the answers.

JAMES THURBER

Keep your hands open, and all the sands of the desert can pass through them. Close them, and all you can feel is a bit of grit.

TAISEN DESHIMARU

A child's world is fresh and new and beautiful, full of wonder and excitement. It is our misfortune that for most of us that clear-eyed vision, that true instinct

for what is beautiful and awe-inspiring,
is dimmed and even lost before we reach
adulthood.

RACHEL CARSON

We are all born charming, fresh, and
spontaneous and must be civilized before
we are fit to participate in society.

MISS MANNERS (JUDITH MARTIN)

How is it that little children are so
intelligent and men so stupid? It must be
education that does it.

ALEXANDRE DUMAS *fils*

Whosoever shall not receive the kingdom of God as a little child shall in no wise enter therein.

LUKE 18:7

There are children playing in the street who could solve some of my top problems in physics, because they have modes of sensory perception that I lost long ago.

J. ROBERT OPPENHEIMER

"Did you have a happy childhood?" is a false question. As a child I did not know what happiness was, and whether I was happy or not. I was too busy *being*.

ALISTAIR REID

You don't need Little League. You don't even need nine kids. Four is plenty—a pitcher, a batter, and a couple of shaggers. You can play ball all day long. My kids used to try to get me out there, but I'd just say, "Go play with your brothers." If kids want to do something, they'll do it. They don't need adults to do it for them.

YOGI BERRA

Once in a while it really hits people that they don't have to experience the world in the way they have been told to.

ALAN KEIGHTLEY

ORDINARY MIND

If you walk, just walk. If you sit, just sit; but whatever you do, don't wobble.

UMMON

The Buddha, the Godhead, resides quite as comfortably in the circuits of a digital computer or the gears of a cycle transmission as he does at the top of a mountain or in the petals of a flower.

Robert Pirsig

In Buddhism there is no place for using effort. Just be ordinary and nothing special. Eat your food, move your bowels, pass water, and when you're tired go and lie down. The ignorant will laugh at me, but the wise will understand.

Rinzai

If a man has nothing to eat, fasting is the most intelligent thing he can do.

Herman Hesse

I have a simple philosophy: Fill what's empty. Empty what's full. Scratch where it itches.

ALICE ROOSEVELT LONGWORTH

Ken Boswell: *I'm in a rut. I can't break myself of the habit of swinging up at the ball.*
Yogi Berra: *Then swing down.*

Learn your lines and don't trip over the furniture.

SPENCER TRACY
(ADVICE TO YOUNG ACTORS)

Stay out of jail.

ALFRED HITCHCOCK
(ADVICE TO YOUNG FILMMAKERS)

Just sit out there and have them go
through the moves. When you see
something you don't like, change it.

JOSHUA LOGAN

(ADVICE TO YOUNG DIRECTORS)

I'm not *expressing* anything. I'm
presenting people moving.

MERCE CUNNINGHAM

I go about looking at horses and cattle.
They eat grass, make love, work when
they have to, bear their young. I am sick
with envy of them.

SHERWOOD ANDERSON

Learn to wish that everything should come to pass exactly as it does.

EPICTETUS

If you are not happy here and now, you never will be.

TAISEN DESHIMARU

God is in the details.

MIES VAN DER ROHE

Details are all there are.

MAEZUMI

Faith and philosophy are air, but events are brass.

HERMAN MELVILLE

The ability to simplify means to eliminate the unnecessary so that the necessary may speak.

HANS HOFMAN

Monk: *Master, I have just entered the monastery, please teach me.*
Joshu *(778–897): Have you eaten your rice?*
Monk: *Yes, I have.*
Joshu: *Then wash your bowl.*
At these words the monk was enlightened.

While washing the dishes one should only be washing the dishes, which means that while washing the dishes one should be completely aware of the fact that one is washing the dishes. At first glance, that might seem a little silly: why put so much stress on a simple thing? But that's precisely the point. The fact that I am standing there and washing these bowls is a wondrous reality. I'm being completely myself, following my breath, conscious of my presence, and conscious of my thoughts and actions. There's no way I can be tossed around mindlessly like a bottle slapped here and there on the waves.

THICH NHAT HANH

When we pay attention, whatever we are doing—whether it be cooking, cleaning or making love—is transformed and becomes part of our spiritual path. We begin to notice details and textures that we never noticed before; everyday life becomes clearer, sharper, and at the same time more spacious.

RICK FIELDS

Reporter: *Were you apprehensive in the twelfth inning?*

Yogi Berra: *No, but I was scared.*

If we live, we live; if we die, we die; if we suffer, we suffer; if we are terrified, we are terrified. There is no problem about it.

ALAN WATTS

While I have been fumbling over books
And thinking about God and the Devil
   and all,
Other young men have been battling
   with the days
And others have been kissing the
   beautiful women.

ALDOUS HUXLEY

Look for knowledge not in books but in things themselves.

WILLIAM GILBERT

It is the familiar that usually eludes us in life. What is before our nose is what we see last.

WILLIAM BARRETT

It requires a certain kind of mind to see beauty in a hamburger bun. Yet, is it any more unusual to find grace in the texture and softly curved silhouette of a bun than to reflect lovingly on . . . the arrangement of textures and colors in a butterfly's wing?

RAY KROC

Sacred cows make great hamburgers.

ROBERT REISNER

There's a certain Buddhistic calm that comes from having . . . money in the bank.

TOM ROBBINS

The aspects of things that are most important for us are hidden because of their simplicity and familiarity.

LUDWIG WITTGENSTEIN

Nansen (748–834) was a disciple of Basso and the teacher of Joshu. The following exchange occurred when Joshu was a young man:

Joshu: *What is the Way?*

Nansen: *Ordinary mind is the Way.*

Joshu: *Shall I seek it?*

Nansen: *No, if you seek it you cannot find it.*

Joshu: *Then how shall I know the Way?*

Nansen: *The Way is not a matter of knowing or not knowing. Knowing is delusion; not knowing is confusion. The true Way is as vast and boundless as outer space. How can you talk about it in terms of right and wrong?*

At this Joshu was enlightened.

I have been waiting twenty years for someone to say to me: "You have to fight fire with fire" so that I could reply, "That's funny—I always use water."

HOWARD GOSSAGE

In what is seen there should be just the seen; in what is heard there should be just the heard; in what is sensed there should be just the sensing; in what is thought there should be just the thought.

THE BUDDHA

I raise my hand; I take a book from the other side of this desk; I hear the boys playing ball outside my window; I see the clouds blown away beyond the neighboring woods;—in all these I am practicing Zen, I am living Zen. No worldly discussion is necessary, or any explanation.

D. T. SUZUKI

This—the immediate, everyday, and present experience—is IT, the entire and ultimate point for the existence of a universe.

ALAN WATTS

Don't let me catch anyone talking about the Universe in my department.

ERNEST RUTHERFORD

NO-MIND

When the mind is nowhere it is everywhere. When it occupies one tenth, it is absent in the other nine tenths.

TAKUAN

Mindfulness is a state wherein one is totally aware in any situation and so always able to respond appropriately. Yet one is aware of being aware. Mindlessness, on the other hand, or "no-mindness" as it has been called, is a condition of such complete absorption that there is no vestige of self-awareness.

PHILIP KAPLEAU

Don't think: Look!

LUDWIG WITTGENSTEIN

When you try to stop activity to achieve passivity your very effort fills you with activity.

SENG TS'AN

The mind of a perfect man is like a mirror. It grasps nothing. It reflects but does not hold. Therefore, the perfect man can act without effort.

CHUANG TZU

The truth of a thing is the feel of it, not the think of it.

STANLEY KUBRICK

More wisdom is latent in things-as-they-are than in all the words men use.

ANTOINE DE SAINT-EXUPÉRY

No one is more liable to make mistakes than the man who acts only on reflection.

MARQUIS DE VAUVENARGUES

The wild geese do not intend to cast their
  reflections,
The water has no mind to receive their
  images.

Zen haiku

Think enough and you won't know
anything.

Kenneth Patchen

How should men know what is coming
to pass within them, when there are no
words to grasp it? How could the drops
of water know themselves to be a river?
Yet the river flows on.

Antoine de Saint-Exupéry

When you are at sea, keep clear of
the land.

Publilius Syrus

In every part and corner of our life, to
lose oneself is to be gainer; to forget
oneself is to be happy.

Robert Louis Stevenson

We can only exist by taking our minds
off the fact that we exist.

Thomas Bernhard

At times I think and at times I am.

Paul Valéry

You think too much, Boss.

The only free mind is one that, pure of
all intimacy with beings or objects, plies
its own vacuity.

E. M. CIORAN

The no-mind not-thinks no-thoughts
about no-things.

THE BUDDHA

When I am working on a problem, I never think about beauty. I only think of how to solve the problem. But when I have finished, if the solution is not beautiful, I know it is wrong.

R. BUCKMINSTER FULLER

The highest purpose is to have no purpose at all. This puts one in accord with nature, in her manner of operation.

JOHN CAGE

People think the Beatles know what's going on. We don't. We're just doing it.

JOHN LENNON

Man, if you gotta ask, you'll never know.

LOUIS ARMSTRONG

(ASKED TO DEFINE JAZZ)

My life has no purpose, no direction, no aim, no meaning, and yet I'm happy. I can't figure it out. What am I doing right?

CHARLES M. SCHULZ

A drunken man who falls out of a cart, though he may suffer, does not die. His bones are the same as other people's, but he meets his accident in a different way. His spirit is in a condition of security. He is not conscious of riding in the cart; neither is he conscious of falling out of it. Ideas of life, death, fear and the like cannot penetrate his breast; and so he does not suffer from contact with objective existence. If such security is to be got from wine, how much more is to be got from God?

CHUANG TZU

How old would you be if you didn't know how old you was?

SATCHEL PAIGE

NOT-TWO

NOTHINGNESS

Clay is molded to make a vessel, but
the utility of the vessel lies in the space
where there is nothing. . . . Thus, taking
advantage of what is, we recognize the
utility of what is not.

LAO TZU

God made everything out of nothing, but
the nothingness shows through.

PAUL VALÉRY

It's the nothing that makes us something,
it's what we miss that hits the mark.

7-UP JINGLE

The game is not about becoming
somebody, it's about becoming nobody.

Baba Ram Dass

Seeing into nothingness—this is the true
seeing, the eternal seeing.

Shen Hui

We put thirty spokes together and call it
   a wheel;
But it is the space where there is nothing
   that the usefulness of the wheel
   depends.
We turn clay to make a vessel;
But it is on the space where there is
   nothing that the usefulness of the
   vessel depends.
We pierce doors and windows to make
   a house;
And it is on these spaces where there is

nothing that the usefulness of the
house depends.
Therefore just as we take advantage
of what is, we should recognize the
usefulness of what is not.

Lao Tzu

It is precisely because there is nothing
within the One that all things are from it.

Plotinus

Apart from the known and the unknown,
what else is there?

Harold Pinter

At a given moment I open my eyes
and exist. And before that, during all
eternity, what was there? Nothing.

UGO BETTI

The unrest which keeps the never
stopping clock of metaphysics going is
the thought that the nonexistence of this
world is just as possible as its existence.

WILLIAM JAMES

Mu: *Literally "no" or "not." Mu signifies
the absence of everything, but it does not
mean "nothing"—it transcends the illusory
distinction between positive and negative and
is sometimes translated as "not two." It is said
that once you have grasped Mu, you have
grasped Zen.*

Every thing is of the nature of no thing.

PARMENIDES

One thing in my defense, not that it matters: I know something Carter never knew, or Helene, or maybe you. I know what "nothing" means, and keep on playing.

JOAN DIDION

I was twenty when I went in, thirty-one when I come out. You don't count months and years—you don't do time that way. You gotta forget time; you gotta not give a fuck if you live or die. You gotta get to where nothin' means nothin'.

JAMES CAAN

(IN Thief, SCREENPLAY BY MICHAEL MANN)

Nothing, like something, happens anywhere.

PHILIP LARKIN

Everything depends on this: a fathomless sinking into a fathomless nothingness.

JOHANNES TAULER

There is nothing to express, nothing with which to express, nothing from which to express, no power to express, no desire to express, together with the obligation to express.

SAMUEL BECKETT

When you have understood that nothing *is*, that things do not even deserve the status of appearances, you no longer need to be saved, you are saved, and miserable for it.

E. M. Cioran

Act non-action; undertake no undertaking; taste the tasteless.

Lao Tzu

How did it come about that beings take precedence everywhere and lay claim to every "is" while that which is not a being is understood as Nothing, though it is Being itself, and remains forgotten?

Martin Heidegger

Expect nothing, and anything seems everything. Expect everything, and anything seems nothing.

SAMUEL HAZO

All Buddhas preach emptiness. Why? Because they wish to crush the concrete ideas of the students. If a student even clings to an idea of emptiness, he betrays all Buddhas.

BODHIDHARMA

I stick my finger into existence—it smells of nothing. Where am I? Who am I? What is this thing called the world? What does this word mean?

SØREN KIERKEGAARD

Tomorrow, and tomorrow, and tomorrow
Creeps in this petty pace from day to day,
To the last syllable of recorded time;
And all our yesterdays have lighted fools
The way to dusty death. Out, out, brief
    candle!
Life's but a walking shadow, a poor
    player
That struts and frets his hour upon the
    stage
And then is heard no more. It is a tale
Told by an idiot, full of sound and fury
Signifying nothing.

WILLIAM SHAKESPEARE
(Macbeth)

What is at the world's end, as at its
beginning, is not the Nothingness which
explains nothing, but God. And this
end must not simply be equated with a
cosmic catastrophe and the sudden end
of human history. What is old, transient,

imperfect, and evil will indeed be ended, but this end must be understood as ultimate completion and fulfillment.

HANS KÜNG

Eternal nothingness is okay if you're dressed for it.

WOODY ALLEN

ONENESS

When we want to understand something, we cannot just stand outside and observe it. We have to enter deeply into it and be one with it in order to really understand. If we want to understand a person, we have to feel his feelings, suffer his sufferings, and enjoy his joy. The word "comprehend" is made up of the Latin root *cum*, which means "with," and *prehendere*, which means "to grasp it or pick it up." To comprehend something means to pick it up and become one with it. There is no other way to understand something. In Buddhism, we call this kind of understanding "non-duality." Not two.

THICH NHAT HANH

Nothing is born, nothing is destroyed. Away with your dualism, your likes and dislikes. Every single thing is just One Mind. When you have perceived this, you will have mounted the Chariot of the Buddhas.

HUANG PO

Whole sight; or all the rest is desolation.

JOHN FOWLES

All numbers are multiples of one, all sciences converge to a common point, all wisdom comes out of one center, and the number of wisdom is one.

PARACELSUS

The truth is that everything is One, and this of course is not a numerical One.

PHILIP KAPLEAU

There is no remainder in the mathematics of infinity. All life is one; therefore, there cannot be God and man, nor a universe and God. A god not in the world is a false god, and a world not in God is unreal. All things return to one, and one operates in all.

NYOGEN SENZAKI

In the "Not Two" are no separate things,
yet all things are included.

Seng Ts'an

Knowledge is one. Its subdivisions
into subjects is a concession to human
weakness.

Sir Halford John Mackinder

All know that the drop merges into
the ocean but few know that the ocean
merges into the drop.

Kabir

Everything in the universe is connected,
everything is osmosis. You cannot
separate any part from the whole:
interdependence rules the cosmic order.

Taisen Deshimaru

The one is none other than the All, the
All none other than the One.

SENG TS'AN

And I have felt . . . a sense sublime
Of something far more deeply interfused,
Whose dwelling is the light of setting
    suns,
And the round ocean and the living air,
And the blue sky, and in the mind of
    man;
A motion and a spirit, that impels
All thinking things, all objects of all
    thought,
And rolls through all things.

WILLIAM WORDSWORTH

The knower and the known are one. Simple people imagine that they should see God, as if He stood there and they here. This is not so. God and I, we are one in knowledge.

MEISTER ECKHART

The highest wisdom has but one science—the science of the whole—the science explaining the whole creation and man's place in it.

LEO TOLSTOY

When you sit in the full lotus position, your left foot is on your right thigh and your right foot is on your left thigh. When we cross our legs like this, even though we have a right leg and a left leg, they have become one. The position expresses the oneness of duality: not two and not one. This is the most important teaching: not two, and not one. Our body and mind are not two and not one. If you think your body and mind are two, that is wrong; if you think that they are one, that is also wrong. Our body and mind are both two *and* one.

SHUNRYU SUZUKI

All beings are Buddha. All beings are the truth, just as they are.

ROBERT AITKEN

SELECT BIBLIOGRAPHY

Aitken, Robert. *Taking the Path of Zen*. San Francisco: North Point Press, 1982.

Baba Ram Dass (Richard Alpert). *Be Here Now*. San Cristobal, NM: Lama Foundation, 1971.

Bancroft, Anne. *Modern Mystics and Sages*. London: Granada, 1978.

————. *Zen: Direct Pointing to Reality*. New York: Thames and Hudson, 1979.

Bell, Peter. "Zen Abuse." *Icon Magazine*, February 1998.

Benares, Camden. *Zen Without Zen Masters*. Berkeley, CA: And/Or Press, 1977.

The Bhagavad Gita. Translated by Eknath Easwaran. Petaluma, CA: Nilgiri Press, 1985.

Blackstone, Judith, and Zoran Josipovic. *Zen for Beginners*. London: Unwin, 1986.

Blofeld, John. *The Zen Teaching of Huang Po*. New York: Grove Press, 1959.

Blyth, R. H. *Games Zen Masters Play*. Edited by Robert Sohl and Audrey Carr. New York: New American Library, 1976.

————. *Zen in English Literature and Oriental Classics*. Tokyo: Hokuseido Press, 1942.

Brandon, David. *Zen in the Art of Helping*. New York: Dell, 1976.

Cage, John. *Silence*. Cambridge, MA: MIT Press, 1966.

————. *A Year from Monday*. Middletown, CT: Wesleyan University Press, 1963.

Capra, Fritjof. *The Tao of Physics*. New York: Bantam, 1977.

————. *Uncommon Wisdom*. New York: Simon and Schuster, 1988.

Cleary, J. C. *Zen Dawn*. Boston: Shambhala, 1986.

Coupland, Douglas. *Generation X*. New York: St. Martin's, 1991.

Deshimaru, Taisen. *Questions to A Zen Master*. Translated by Nancy Amphoux. New York: Dutton, 1961.

————. *The Ring of the Way: The Testament of a Zen Master*. Compiled by Evelyn de Smedt and Dominique Dussaussoy. Translated by Nancy Amphoux. New York: Dutton, 1983.

————. *The Zen Way to the Martial Arts*. Translated by Nancy Amphoux. New York: Dutton, 1982.

Dumoulin, Heinrich. *Zen Enlightenment: Origins and Meaning*. Translated by John C. Maraldo. New York: Weatherhill, 1976.

Dürckheim, Karlfried Graf. *Zen and Us.* New York: Dutton, 1987.

Eliot, Alexander. *Zen Edge.* New York: Seabury Press, 1979.

Eliot, T. S. *The Cocktail Party.* London: Faber, 1974.

Fast, Howard. *The Art of Zen Meditation.* Culver City, CA: Peace Press, 1977.

Fields, Rick, with Peggy Taylor, Rex Weyler, and Rick Ingrasci. *Chop Wood, Carry Water.* Los Angeles: Tarcher, 1984.

Fromm, Erich, D. T. Suzuki, and Richard De Martino. *Zen Buddhism and Psychoanalysis.* New York: Harper & Row, 1970.

Gallwey, W. Timothy. *The Inner Game of Tennis.* New York: Random House, 1974.

Green, Michael. *Zen and the Art of the Macintosh.* Philadelphia: Running Press, 1986.

Hammitzsch, Horst. *Zen in the Art of the Tea Ceremony.* New York: Avon, 1980.

Hanh, Thich Nhat. *The Miracle of Mindfulness.* Boston: Beacon Press, 1975.

————. *Peace Is Every Step.* New York: Bantam, 1991.

Harding, D. E. *On Having No Head.* London: Arkana, 1986.

Haskel, Peter. *Bankei Zen.* Edited by Yoshito Hakeda. New York: Grove Press, 1984.

Herrigel, Eugen. *The Method of Zen.* New York: Pantheon, 1960.

————. *Zen in the Art of Archery.* New York: Pantheon, 1953.

Herrigel, Gustie L. *Zen in the Art of Flower Arrangement.* Translated by R. F. C. Hall. London: Routledge & Kegan Paul, 1958.

Hesse, Herman. *Siddhartha.* New York: New Directions, 1951.

Humphreys, Christmas. *Walk On!* Wheaton, IL: Theosophical Publishing, 1974.

————. *A Western Approach to Zen.* Wheaton, IL: Theosophical Publishing, 1971.

————. *Zen, A Way of Life.* Boston: Little, Brown, 1962.

Hyams, Joe. *Zen in the Martial Arts.* New York: Bantam, 1982.

Huxley, Aldous. *The Doors of Perception.* New York: Harper & Row, 1970.

————. *The Perennial Philosophy.* New York: Harper & Row, 1945.

Jackson, Phil, and Hugh Delehanty. *Sacred Hoops: Spiritual Lessons of a Hardwood Warrior.* New York: Hyperion, 1995.

Jung, C. G. *The Collected Works of C. G. Jung.* Translated by R. F. C. Hull. Princeton: Princeton University Press, 1959.

Kapleau, Philip. *The Three Pillars of Zen.* Garden City, NY: Doubleday, 1980.

Kasulis, T. P. *Zen Action, Zen Person.* Honolulu: University of Hawaii Press, 1985.

Keightley, Alan. *Into Every Life a Little Zen Must Fall.* London: Wisdom Publications, 1986.

Krishnamurti, Jiddu. *Talks and Dialogues.* New York: Avon, 1970.

Küng, Hans. *Why I Am Still A Christian.* Nashville: Abingdon, 1987.

Leggett, Trevor. *A First Zen Reader.* Rutland, VT: Tuttle, 1960.

————. *The Warrior Koans.* London: Arkana, 1985.

————. *Zen and the Ways.* Rutland, VT: Tuttle, 1987.

Linssen, Robert. *Living Zen.* Translated by Diana Abrahams-Curiel. New York: Grove Press, 1958.

Maezumi, Hakuyu Taizan, and Bernard Tetsugen Glassman. *The Hazy Moon of Enlightenment.* Los Angeles: Zen Center Publications, 1977.

Matthiessen, Peter. *Nine-Headed Dragon River.* Boston: Shambhala, 1987.

Merton, Thomas. *Zen and the Birds of Appetite.* New York: New Directions, 1963.

Murphy, Michael, and Rhea W. White. *The Psychic Side of Sports.* Reading, MA: Addison-Wesley, 1978.

Perry, Whitall N. *A Treasury of Traditional Wisdom.* New York: Harper & Row, 1986.

Pirsig, Robert M. *Zen and the Art of Motorcycle Maintenance.* New York: Morrow, 1974.

Reps, Paul. *Zen Flesh, Zen Bones.* Rutland, VT: Tuttle, 1957.

Rosen, Gerald. *Zen in the Art of J. D. Salinger.* Berkeley: Creative Arts, 1977.

Ross, Nancy Wilson. *The World of Zen.* New York: Vintage, 1960.

Russell, Bertrand. *Philosophical Essays.* London: Allen & Unwin, 1966.

Sangharakshita, Maha Sthavira. *The Essence of Zen.* Glasgow: Windhorse, 1985.

Schloegl, Irmgard. *The Wisdom of the Zen Masters.* New York: New Directions, 1976.

Sekida, Katsuki. *Two Zen Classics:* Mumonkan *and* Hekiganroku. Edited by A. V. Grimstone. New York: Weatherhill, 1977.

Senzaki, Nyogen, and Ruth Strout McCandless. *Buddhism and Zen*. San Francisco: North Point Press, 1987.

Shakespeare, William. *Hamlet*. New Haven: Yale, 2003.

———. *Macbeth*. New York: Penguin, 2000.

Shaku, Shoyen. *Zen for Americans*. Translated by Daisetz Teitaru Suzuki. LaSalle, IL: Open Court, 1974.

Shibayama, Zenkei. *A Flower Does Not Talk*. Translated by Sumiko Kudo. Rutland, VT: Tuttle, 1970.

Sohl, Robert, and Audrey Carr. *The Gospel According to Zen*. New York: New American Library, 1970.

Soho, Takuan. *The Unfettered Mind*. Translated by William Scott Wilson. Tokyo: Kodansha, 1986.

Suzuki, Daisetz Teitaro. *The Awakening of Zen*. Edited by Christmas Humphreys. Boston: Shambhala, 1987.

———. *What is Zen?* New York: Harper & Row, 1972.

———. *Zen Buddhism*. Edited by William Barrett. New York: Doubleday, 1956.

Suzuki, Shunryu. *Zen Mind, Beginner's Mind*. Edited by Trudy Dixon. New York: Weatherhill, 1970.

Trungpa, Chögyam. *Shambhala: The Sacred Path of the Warrior*. New York: Bantam, 1986.

Tzu, Lao. *Tao Te Ching*. Translated by D. C. Lau. New York: Penguin, 1963.

Van de Wetering, Janwillem. *The Empty Mirror*. Boston: Houghton Mifflin, 1975.

Vonnegut, Kurt. *Slaughterhouse Five*. New York: Delacorte, 1969.

Watanabe, Teresa. "It's Now, It's Zen, and It's Life-Changing." *Los Angeles Times*, June 1, 2004.

Watts, Alan. *The Spirit of Zen*. New York: Grove Press, 1960.

———. *This Is It*. New York: Vintage, 1973.

———. *The Way of Zen*. New York: Pantheon, 1957.

Wittgenstein, Ludwig. *Philosophical Investigations*. Translated by G. E. M. Anscombe. Oxford: Blackwell, 1953.

———. *Remarks on the Foundations of Mathematics*. Translated by G. E. M. Anscombe. Oxford: Blackwell, 1978.

Wood, Ernest. *Zen Dictionary*. Rutland, VT: Tuttle, 1972.

INDEX

ABOUT THE AUTHOR

Jon Winokur lives in Pacific Palisades, California.